THE SECRET OF SPEY

THE CAVE OF RAITTS

(page 45)

THE SECRET OF SPEY

BY

WENDY WOOD

*WITH ILLUSTRATIONS
BY THE AUTHOR*

EDINBURGH
ROBERT GRANT & SON
126 PRINCES STREET

First Published 1930

Printed in Great Britain by T. and A. Constable Ltd.
at the University Press, Edinburgh

FOREWORD

LACKING especial gifts, descriptive, analytical, and topographical, no writer can well hope to express a region through the written word, to unveil its intimacies, or comprehend the genius of its atmosphere and folk-mind; and it is just because Miss Wendy Wood is so temperamentally adapted to such a task that she has in the following pages succeeded so admirably in providing us with a comprehensive study and panorama of Speyside. To put a province into a book so that one may place a finger on the model and miniature of mountain, glen, or road is assuredly one of the gifts magical, and happy is the reader who has ever beside him a holiday in printed pages such as is this volume, to which he may turn again and yet again in the certainty of breathing captive breezes and wandering enchanted braesides in the brogues of imagination.

Why Speyside should have been so comparatively neglected heretofore I do not know. But I do know that this is the day and season of the making good of omissions, of the ardent search for lands still uncharted in the mappamound of letters. In the present instance the explorer is so manifestly a guide naturally born, that doubts cannot be enter-tained regarding the authenticity of her method. A natural hill-climber and pedestrian to whom mountains have a personality only to be understood through the intimacy of ascent, an unrepentant devotee of moorlands, wandering the most remote unescorted and unafraid, a knowledgeable folk-loreist and comradely friend of Tinklers and Gypsies, Miss Wood has in her itinerary of this familiar yet unchronicled region given us the key and sesame we needed for its full understanding. She has indeed dealt with it so faithfully that to visit it without reading this book will be as stupid as visiting Wales without reading Borrow, or the Balkans without first perusing Martinengo-Cesaresco.

To my way of thinking, the chief charm of these pages resides in the manner in which Miss Wood deals with the legends and folk-beliefs of Speyside, recounting and explaining each tale or freit in association with its appropriate scene. But her word-pictures of the varied scenery of Speyside will, I believe, make an even stronger appeal to the majority of Scots readers, who, after all, are much more intrigued by the sublimities of their own land than many credit them with being. Nor will they find here a trace of the School of Baedeker, father of topographical clichés, and they will look in vain for the instructions of the dragoman to cast their eyes right and left in search of " places of interest." Miss Wood may indeed be said to have rescued local travel from the terrors of the nudging elbow. Nor are exclamation marks necessary to the conveyance of her information.

The entire history of regional expression and explication makes it most plain that unless it be undertaken by precisely the right sort of person it will fail of its purpose. The few writers who have made a success of it have been those who found it as natural and instinctive as the swift her spring flight. And when I say that I believe Miss Wood to be of these, surely I give you the best of all possible reasons for reading her very charming book.

LEWIS SPENCE.

CONTENTS

ILLUSTRATIONS

FULL PAGE

IN TEXT

LOCH EANAICH

(page 30)

THE SECRET OF SPEY

THERE is no more deceitful handbook than a map. Not only because its village roofs are invisible, its forests flat, its crinkly burns silent and the contours of its ravines unshadowed, but because it does not indicate the mind of the country, the interwoven memory and experience of it, which a blind man might gather though his eyes never beheld the hills nor knew a turn of the road.

It is not only the deception of scale, though I have every sympathy with the exhausted climber who wearily scanned the mapped miles, and seeing a tiny beetle take Ben MacDhui in three strides, annihilated the competitor in sudden wrath. There is a further misunderstanding, for that which on the map looks like a little clachan may turn out to be a nest of Victorian villas; or a road that looks uninviting on the flat of paper may prove to open on a series of magnificent views, while a track that suggests solitude may in reality be marred by the insistent company of telegraph poles; indeed, some places seem deliberately to deceive even on actual acquaintance and wear a disguise for the mockery of visitors.

Speyside at first appears no more than " the beautiful road to Inverness," with petrol pumps at convenient intervals and mountains that focus well from the front seat of a car. Such a road shows the forests, but misses the sound of the wind that moves unceasingly among the pine-tops like the deep voice of the outer ocean; shows churches, but misses so often the clang of their little bells, misses the kindly tongue of the secluded people and the tangled tales that lie among the strata of the years; and yet —even lacking all this intimacy, a passing glimpse of the strath of the Spey is impressive and lovely.

Stream and waterfall tumble from great hills on every hand: hills near enough to the byways to invite with their secret corries or frank heights, and yet just far enough away to send out their beauty without the coldness of their shadows and to hold the enchantment of distance.

On the south-east the blue peaks of the Cairn-gorm range or Monadh Ruadh ramp with sudden splendour; sometimes majestically suspended as an Atlantic wave above the wide valley, sometimes entirely lost in mist. The Grey or Monadhliath hills, comfortable in forest cloak, brood north-westward, while the south is blocked by the Gramp-ians, whose black turrets cut the blazing sunsets.

In spring and summer, Speyside is flower-covered. Purple gentian, bluebell, golden lady's-straw, violas, vetch and clover intermingle with all the impossible glory of a Morris chintz; and through the beauty, like an emblem on a pictorial map, winds the black serpent of the Spey.

It is strange that a river of such definite character should not have been given a more interesting name. The designation may be akin to the word " spate," but not to within a few miles of the river's mouth is the term applicable. Ptolemy's map of A.D. 150

marks it as " Tuessis," a variation of " Taua," a latinised form of Tay, simply meaning—a river.

The Spey is the most eccentric among rivers. It has no lovable banks, it neither chortles over stones nor fights with rocks. It has no song. What a condemnation! Instead of singing, it grumbles and mumbles as it swirls uselessly along to Grantown. Always alluded to as " she," the Spey, like many a woman whose strength of character is more obvious than her beauty, gains in respect and fear what she loses in admiration. In few places are the remains of river-worship so obvious. It is still a saying in the vicinity that her waters demand one life a year. In this she is certainly less greedy than the Dee,

> " Bloodthirsty Dee
> Each year needs three,"

or even the Till, for,

> " Said Tweed to Till,
> ' Whit gars ye rin sae still ? '
> Till said to Tweed,
> ' Though ye rin wi' speed
> An' I rin slaw,
> Whaur ye droon ae man
> I droon twa.' "

For all the modesty of her demands, the Spey often gets more than her requirements. Unwary visitors, mistakenly confident of their boating and swimming powers, impatient natives at fords or on insecure bridges, and over-enthusiastic fishers pay toll year after year. Warning seems useless, for the treacherous under-current which is the real danger is discernible only at certain points, and it is hard to believe that the smooth patches above the submerged whirlpools do not betoken good behaviour. The old MacFarlane Manuscript says of the river : " You might judge it fordable.   Far uthair wayis. It is a great deal more deep than it doth show ! " The best method of giving a Safety First exhibition is to throw a tree trunk into the water.   Its immediate and complete disappearance is as astonishing as it is impressive.   What wonder folks believed in a devouring spirit that haunted the river !

" Who is so foolish as to talk now of the White Horse of Spey ? ' said an old lady to me.   " Dear me !   That 's old talk ;   but all the same she 's a bad, bad river."

Though white horses figure in Celtic Faerie Tales, the colour is unusual for the Kelpie or Capall ;   but the beautiful beast of Spey behaved according to tradition in all other respects.   Particularly on stormy nights it was to be seen, when the clouds raced over the face of the moon, throwing the whole countryside into shadow one moment, and the next flooding it with the silver light that shows the detail of every twig.   The great white horse, sleek, and dainty in its stepping, bedecked with fine trappings, would walk beside the weary traveller. Sometimes it whinnied softly, nuzzling its velvet nose into the pedestrian's hand, and questioning with the gentle deeps of its large eyes.

Those who know what it is to be footsore to the point of dropping, and who know also the lovableness of a horse, will understand how wayfarers who

had even been warned of the danger of such a ride
would at last mount the White Horse of Spey.
Once mounted, the traveller immediately rued his
act. No gentle whinnyings now! No pretty
curvetings! With an eldrich scream the steed
broke into full gallop, mane and tail streaming in
the wind of the pace, while the terror-stricken rider
strove ever harder to free himself from the spell that
bound him to the creature's back as they neared the
gleam of the river. The uninterrupted dash ended
in a plunge—a splash—leaving nothing but the
echo of a triumphant song to signify that the Kelpie
had another victim to devour at his leisure.

The song of the Horse as I heard it was only
fragmentary,

> " Ride you,
> Ride me,
> Kelpie,
> Creavie,"

but Mr. MacPherson gives : [1]

> " And ride weel, Davie,
> And by this night at ten o'clock
> Ye 'll be in Pot Cravie."

The surname of this Davie may be guessed as
being Jones, since that gentleman, under various
disguises, had charge over water devils who brought
bodies for his " Locker," or in this case to Pot
Cravie.

Though the river only runs through one loch
between Kingussie and Grantown, the strath is a

[1] *Primitive Beliefs in the North-East of Scotland,* J. M. MacPherson.

southern echo of the Great Glen of the North, and would also be a chain of lochs if silting and sinking levels had not reduced it to land again. It is still by no means " dry " land. The marsh between Ruthven and Insh is crossed by an embankment to support the railway, which is further safeguarded by false banks to keep the Spey in bounds. In spite of these precautions, heavy rainfall or sudden melting of snow transforms the valley to an inland sea, and the inhabitants have many an unwelcome illustration of the primitive condition of the land and the reason for its earliest population having lived high upon the hillsides.

" If you had seen this place at the time of the flood of 1829, you would not have seen anything but water all up and down, and down and up the way," said Archie. " It was nothing but the little knolls that stuck out of the water, or the tops of trees."

Archie is not much over eighty, but stories of the Great Storm of '29 must have been supped with his first spoonful of brose, and intimacy with the very streams that wrought devastation has quickened his imagination and perhaps kept apprehension alive, for he reckons the passing of time as if he were a son of Noah himself.

" It would be fifteen years after the flood " serves as preamble to many of his stories, or he may ring the changes on " At the time of the flood it would be "; and it took me a little while to realise that in speaking of his predecessors as " born before the flood " he was not referring to antediluvian ancestry.

Sir Thomas Dick Lauder says that the storm was

heralded by " Twa suns in the sky." Perhaps the nature of such a vision precluded it from being taken seriously ; at any rate little attention was paid to it, and the forty-two hours of incessant rain and excessive wind that followed wrought havoc the whole length of the valley. Householders floated about on " branders " or rafts with their household goods, or shared islets a couple of ells long with terrified hares and rabbits. Bridges burst and mills crashed into the swirling torrents and added the battering-rams of their fallen timber to the force of the water to wrench cottages from the tottering banks.

Repetitions have occurred, but on a mercifully small scale, and a departmental rainbow is now visible in the scheme to utilise the surplus waters of the Spey for the electrical supply. In this way, not only would the fear of flood be removed, but good loam land which is at present only the haunt of ragged-robin and mosquitoes could be ablow with corn.

Good land is precious, as a glance at any well-tended field in winter will show ; for the soil is covered, not, as at first appears, with an outsize potato crop waiting to be lifted, but with large round stones, multitudinous, innumerable, like the scene of some impossible task requiring an elfin agency to clear it. The sound of the driven ploughshare gives, not the fruity swish of turning loam, but a continuous scritch and scrape in accompaniment to the occasional " clack " of a horse's hoof striking a stone. In this gravelly bed nothing but potatoes, oats, and turnips can be grown. To balance this disadvantage, the pasturage is good, especially on the lower hills, and for that reason it is all the more surprising to see the farmers' wives and house-keepers taking supplies of Danish butter, margarine, and Dutch cheese from the visiting grocers' vans, while the reason for this anomaly looks over the stone dyke in the shape of a pranksome calf, old enough to be trying its " corns " on everything, and most certainly old enough to be seeking its own food instead of taking sustenance from its mother and leaving the farm with no milk to " lashgielavie " as they say in the West. But pride of calf comes first, and every one is satisfied if the young ne'er-do-weel is maturing for the meat market.

Down the ages the meat market has been the mainstay of this countryside; from the heterogene-ous collection of the cateran, to the prize herds of the Laird of Rothiemurchus which were the wonder of his Herefordshire estate. Not that the English shire was given much opportunity of admiring the cattle that were so patiently herded South by the shepherd of Grant, for the old man, unused to hedged pastures, put his charges to rest overnight in a field surrounded by yew, and in the morning the famous herd lay dead of poisoning.

The names of farms on the banks of the Spey incorporating the word " gour," a goat, make one wonder at the scarcity of those satyric creatures. No one is more thankful than I that the pleasant difficulties of mountain-climbing are not rendered more exciting by a possible encounter with an oblique-eyed son of Satan, but in a district where visitors have to book their milk months beforehand goats' milk and cheese would surely be useful to eke out the supply. I have spoken to those who remember seeing wild goats on the Cairngorm range, and know of letters between landlords and tenants proving that goats were, up to twenty years ago, kept—one might say " very persistently " kept —on the hillsides, but they were finally removed because they interfered with the shooting.

Other things have been removed also, as the extraordinary number of ruined clachans show. Their ghost-fields stand out emerald-green among the surrounding heather and blaeberry, telling with more insistency than written word or speech the tale of a lost people.

So Speyside welcomes the visitor, and mixes financial necessity with the old Highland hospitality. Even if you appear unexpectedly in a mackintosh that has weathered a hundred storms and gathered some stain from every rocky shelter and mossy seat in the North ; even if you are loaded with a haver-sack that appears to hold all that is worthless, while the extra pair of muddy shoes at your belt would cause your nearest relative to put you from the door, on Speyside you will be offered refreshment before you can ask for it, and it will be everybody's concern that you find comfort for the night.

Continuous faithfulness to the beauties of the Cairngorm or Monadh Ruadh range will open the cottage doors ; and if the ancestry of your mind is Highland, the little doors of precious memory will open too, so that you may share the sight of teased wool on the flagstone floor and hear the sound of the wheel and the remnants of old tales that hung to rafters now covered with lath and plaster. You may know the fear of the faerie folk and the dread of witches, and gradually become an intimate relation to every burn and glen, knowing the name within the name which is the endearment and the tale.

It is as well to be thus fortified against the jars of modern life, for progress at present is incongruously erratic rather than gradual. It seems strange for instance, that those who are born and bred beside the mountains do not climb them except from necessity. A stray sheep, the shooting, or attention to high plantations take their respective devotees up the hills quite as often as they wish ; so that on holidays one does not meet the shepherd, forester, or farmhand heading for some peak with a magnificent view ; one meets them instead riding motor-cycles (those new to the machine wearing an expression of delighted terror) towards the nearest village. But those who see the great bens with unaccustomed eyes, distant in the deceiving light of morning or in the magic of sunset, will always feel the pull towards the forest paths that lead to the dramatic summits.

From Kingussie to Cromdale the Cairngorm mountains dominate the scene and the minds of the people. The houses face the hills, are named after the hills, and if the visitor is capable of putting one foot before the other, he will be urged to go to the hills. Indeed the lame are not exempt. I have heard tales that vie with the claims of Lourdes ; examples of rheumatic cripples who arrived on crutches and who finally ascended Braeriach— pushed there, I believe, by the mental persistence of the village inhabitants !

No native is content until the visitor has returned from the edge of some snow-curved precipice that hangs above the world.   Tales of the prowess of former visitors will be skilfully introduced and applauded, and instructions and sandwiches are always ready to hand at the first whispered enquiry. Not that these persistent ladies know the places which they praise ; for, once the snows begin to melt from the foot-hills, the womenfolk have too much to do in preparation for the summer letting to go far afield.

In early spring, blankets blow on every fence, mattresses adorn the green plot, sheets are aspread on the heather like lost snow patches, and little nieces appear on holiday from town service to give a hand with odd duties.

On the land itself preparation is also afoot.   The flood of cleansing burn, the clustering of flower and foliage bud, the slow rising of emerald blade, the green mist among the larches, and the scent of new pine and birch suggest that Nature is joining with the housewives of Spey to display the treasures of the strath.

THE WINDING WAYS

EVERY road should be the great-grandchild of a footpath; something precious born of the thoughts and footprints of our ancestors, whatever changes of size or surface it has to undergo to suit modern needs.

Peaceful people, even when they had the tools, always preferred to go round a hill rather than over or through a hill; it is the conquering hero who must get straight there on a road so clear that ambush is impossible. The Romans made such unimaginative highways, and the Turks cut New Street right through the heart of Old Bagdad, like the precise gash of a shop assistant's scissors through a piece of priceless tapestry.

Now that motorists also want a straight road with no possibility of ambush in the shape of by-path collisions, the old roads are undergoing modification; a corner cut here, a twist widened there, all adding to the ease of driving and the encouragement of transport, but certainly taking from the charm of travel.

In certain places between Perth and Inverness four parallel roads are visible: Wade's road, the turf track that the old folks preferred to his hard highway, the deviations of the road that improved on Wade's foundations, and the new straight cuts that cross the little old curves, wandering beside them like the lost ringlets of an Eton crop.

The introduction of roads into the Highlands was resented by the Chiefs of that time, who were afraid that Lowland influence would weaken the loyalty of the Clans and that their own strongholds would become dangerously accessible. The work of the Great North Road was enlivened, but hardly hindered, by skirmishes with dirk and sgian dubh, for the attacks by small bands of Highlanders were as nothing to a General who defied the climate and moved mountains.

The present-day cubic abominations of cement and whitewash that span the burns are an insult to the glens and to the memory of the First Contractor. Wade's bridges combined durability with beauty; and being made with primitive tools and of local material, were kith to the boulder-strewn mounds and monumental hills. The Irish Field-Marshal must have had some magnetic force to keep his subalterns hard at work vying with each other on different stretches of the wild intractable land. There are places on Speyside where it is easy to see at a glance what a day's road-work must have entailed : the levering of rocks and carrying of boulders, throwing foundations across bogs or collecting little rocks to bridge mountain burns; and at night the lonesome shelter of huts standing isolated in the vast darkness of moorland, no sound to be heard but the cry of the curlew or the drip of moisture from the roughly constructed roofs.

The Privates on road-work earned an extra sixpence a day, the Sergeants a shilling, and the Officers received an extra half-crown, out of which they had to provide themselves with sheds and food. The General paid frequent visits to the different scenes of operation, and as his advent was usually preceded by increased rations, he was quite a welcome figure among his men.

This did not mean that he found favour else-where; indeed the Laird of Rothiemurchus, though a Royalist, found himself honoured too frequently with the General's company, and finally determined to rid his house of a boring guest.

As they sat alone one night in the study at the Doune, the Laird ascertained with conspicuous precaution that no listeners were near, and having locked the door, he whispered to his guest that he knew enough of the General now to offer a toast to his liking, namely, " The King "—and his wineglass passed over the water carafe!

The ruse was quite successful. The military road-maker retreated, and did not again offer to grace the house where his presence might be mis-understood.

The northern road on Speyside is part of Wade's highway to Inverness, but it disagrees at intervals with the plan of the old General, taking a different route at Newtonmore and at Carr Bridge, and also near Lynchat beside Kingussie, where by wandering through a gate you may find the little ghost-road of 1729. Beyond Dunachton it rambles past an open quarry (where the rocks of mica silver look as if their molten pourings had only been arrested by your glance), and rising obscurely, enters a wood and becomes grassy underfoot.

In early May, when the silver birches stand

among their own suspended showers of green rain, and the lambs are as white as new bread, and the blue waters of Loch Insh glimmer through the trees, it is a faerie scene. A scene in which the clumps of mossy boulders scattered through the wood are suggestive of the ruins of Red Riding Hood's home or the House of the Three Bears. If curiosity leads you from the track, you discover that the ground is covered with moss so thick, so deep, that it resembles a green feather-bed into which the foot sinks above the ankle. Not that it would make a satisfactory resting-place, for, apart from the damp, the ant-hills are too numerous. Some of the hummocks, made entirely of birch twigs nipped to a uniform length of about half an inch, reach a height of three feet; others are so low that it is easy to step on them unexpectedly and be suddenly conscious of the full attack of a Lilliputian army. Such an experience brings a hasty desire to be on the unadorned road once more, but this is easier said than done, for in a wood where each birch tree is as extraordinary in shape as the one before, a small green winding track is singularly hard to find.

A little farther on, the wood and road have been cut through by the plough, and a brown field lies before you like a page torn out of a story-book, so there is nothing to do but " make it up " for that page, and find the continuation of the track on the other side, where it brings you down gently to the commonplaces of the main road again.

Another earnest road-maker was James Grant of Grant, who gave directions to his factor in 1764 to make arrangements for quarries to be opened to

supply metal for roads, because he was particularly
anxious to encourage the new wheel carriages for
transport instead of the usual method of suspending
goods from the horses' backs in willow, leather, or
wooden panniers.   The baskets that were then in
use for fertilising the fields were fashioned with
hinged lids at the foot to discharge the load, and the
mention thirty years later of kellachs, which were
cone-shaped baskets slung between wooden wheels,
does not give the impression of great advance in the
carriage trade.   The people indeed complained to
the Laird of Grant that the stones of the new roads
lodged themselves in their horses' hoofs and were
hard on their own feet, and they continued ob-
stinately to use the old tracks between mill and
moor, leaving the new roads untrodden.

Long before their day, however, a king's highway
ran across Tulloch, for Alexander II. caused a road
to be made reaching up to Findhorn.   It was known
at one time as the Via Regia, and later as the Rathad
an Righ, the King's road.

Every glen has a right and a wrong direction of
approach.   One would imagine in some of them
that the Artist had created the scenery from entirely
one point of view.   It is best to enter Badenoch
where road, rail, and river burst through the dark
gates of the Grampians.   From Newtonmore,
journey alongside the Spey, past Loch Insh, past
Loch Alvie, round the foot of Craigellachie, on
through the woods and up to Carr Bridge.   From
there across moorland to Grantown and back by
Abernethy on a little track that winds and curls
among plantations, with the uprising idealism of

RUTHVEN BARRACKS

(page 38)

the Monadh Ruadh like a tapestry background; past little lochs that hide in juniper woods, by the silver birches of Ord Ban, and on over the open moor to face the wilds of Feshie.

It was on this road that, unsure of my way to a certain farm, I enquired of a roadman breaking metal, "Straight on to so and so?" "No, no, very curving—curving all the way," was the reply. On this road all little things seem to have found a congenial home. On the big road the cottages have added attics and the Post Offices are official affairs, but on the curly road the cottages are still low and couthy, and I know of at least one Post Office where there is no room for a customer if full mail-bags have just come in; but as you are in a private house anyway, Granny says you may use the table to write a card if you don't hinder "the bairns getting on with their tea, for they are hungry after school, and will you not take a cup yourself?"

From Kingussie to four miles above Aviemore there are no other roads, except cross-roads between the two banks, and even they are hardly more than elongated bridges, and bridges are too scarce. I wonder would they continue to be so if a return were made to the Church's custom of using the fines imposed upon evil-doers as payment to any proprietor who was prepared to build bridges? The money was handed over on condition that "the delinquents may not be employed in the work and that the bridges be worth the money."[1]

There are long tracks to the shooting-lodges, and there are the smallest and the loveliest of all—the

[1] *In the Shadow of Cairngorm*, Dr. Forsyth.

forest paths. One may wander them at will, free from the repelling arms of fences, free from oversight and the authority of notice-boards. "Trespass" seems to be a word unknown on Speyside. I cannot remember a domineering notice between Grantown and Kingussie.

The result of this freedom is not that it makes the place seem to belong to oneself, but that the forest trails, like the little roads of Cloonagh, "go rambling through your heart," and something of the old-time loyalty and affection for the Owner Chiefs is roused in recognition of their kinship with all nature-loving Scots.

On the big road, the tea-rooms and garages sound the seasons at intervals like an alarm clock, but on the eastern road nothing strikes the time, and it is quite disquieting to meet an occasional car carefully nosing round corners where one quite naturally expected a coach, though the new road was the coaching trail between Perth and Inverness, and before that the mails missed Speyside and went from Edinburgh to Aberdeen and Inverness. At that time a postal runner took the letters from Inverness to Grantown, and from there they were delivered by private runners attached to the most important houses.

Then the Inns were places of importance. They were coach-stable, hotel, Post Office, and the general news-centre of the district. From them sped tales, false or true, to all outlying cottages and farms. The Inn at Lynwilg, which is one of the old Stages, is modern on an old foundation, but the original Inn at Aviemore where Robert Burns was enter-tained is still inhabited; a fine building, putting present-day hotels to shame, if they can be shamed, by its tall dignity, its simplicity of mass, the proportion and decoration of its white gables.

A coach ran also from Grantown to Tomintoul and via Braemar to Perth. Imagine, after the hazard of the journey through the wild mountains between Tomintoul and Braemar, facing the black peril of the narrow Devil's Elbow in Glen Beag! One wonders how the gaily painted wheels and high-curving springs survived this journey over a road so rough that it would not be marked as a track on a modern map. The passengers also must surely have been contrived of sturdy material.

If admiration is due the travellers, it is even more deserved by the drivers. These northern emulators of Hippolytus manœuvred a swaying coach on narrow roads where unstable boulders deflected the wheels, often edging an abyss or pressing through blinding mists that obscured even the leaders of the four-in-hand. The accident that overtook the Grant coach at Feshie might well have kept cautious souls at home for many a day.

On that occasion, the horses, though still in the traces, had the bits out of their mouths while they were being watered, when all of a sudden a herd of pigs came careering round the corner of the Inn and knocked down a ladder that had been standing against the wall. The startled horses set off at full speed towards the bridge over the Feshie; the bridge had no parapets, the wheels went over the side, and the phaeton fell down the steep rocky banks to the bed of the river. The landlord, who

had rushed after, arrived in time to save the Laird
by catching hold of his heel as he was disappearing
over the brink; he was severely injured, but the
lady was killed. Of course this dramatic event was
nothing to a modern 'bus accident, but at least we
have the choice of a train until the next railroad
accident, and can revert from one type of vehicle
to another according to our momentary anxiety,
whereas there was only one choice in the mode of
travel when the Caledonian coach ran three times
a week between Inverness and Perth.

We have our advantages. Our feet do not rustle
in straw, we are not bruised black and blue, nor
deafened by windows that chatter like mad castañets;
but we miss the fun of the old coach—the restive
horses, the difficult stowing of the luggage, the eager
envy and interest of the onlookers, the thrilling
send-off among shouts accompanied by the hollow
" kerlollop " of the horses' hoofs, and the rumble
of the wheels that did not quite serve to deafen the
coachman's high-voiced encouragement or dis-
paragement of his team. Men set off now for
Central Africa with less disturbance and thrill than
the natives of Badenoch experienced when they
boldly faced a journey to Perth.

The six-wheel 'buses with " London-Inverness "
inscribed on their gleaming slats are no more in
touch with the countryside than a Transatlantic
airship is in touch with the fishes; but the local
'buses are another matter. You may travel on
Speyside by the broad or the long 'bus, and to go
even a small journey is to learn much of many
homely affairs.

An extra rattle of windows, the sound of jumping foot-boards accompanied by the scraping ratchet of the brake lever, is the prelude to a halt because the driver has caught sight of a piece of material thrown over a fence or a gate. It is a nondescript drapery which turns out on closer inspection to have once been a Union Jack or Scottish Standard. Only the driver, who has stopped at its behest for years, knows by memory the original device which snow and rain have smeared into a dull grey streaked with muddy reds. He waits. After a minute, during which there is no sign of life from the little house, he toots his horn, and a puzzled-looking hen, its tail-rudder askew in the wind, strolls through the hedge and passes decorously behind the 'bus. The passengers survey the miscellaneous packages that encumber the rear of the vehicle to see if any are labelled for the house and might therefore be disgorged upon the roadside. The driver stares dreamily into the distance, occasionally tooting and turning his head momentarily towards the house, and back to his dreams. Presently a man appears at the gate and hands a note to the driver with a full description of its contents and instructions for its delivery. A remark is made about the hen, and a discussion on poultry follows in which everybody joins as the 'bus rolls on.

The next stop is to pick up a little figure plodding along with a milk-can : "Come and have a ride, Jean," and a shy child with riotous red curls climbs in, using her hands on the steps to assure the safety of the can. Not bold enough to face the passengers, she cuddles to the driver's elbow, and the next traveller being of the same species, they sit together on the three-inch triangle which is all that is left of the driver's seat. The byreman is waiting for the sack of seed potatoes for the Manse and gives news of the cow—and the 'bus rolls on.

There is no need of a bell in the 'bus, it automatically stops at each passenger's destination, more surely than a coster's donkey at a public-house. It seems to slow down of its own accord that the driver may wave his hand to workers in the fields or shout messages of condolence to cottagers for whom he has no parcel. On the last journey homeward it bounces hilariously round the corners, skimming round the edge of Loch Alvie, with nothing but a gold band of the magic ragweed between it and the shimmering waters, taking the bridges with a contented little rumble, and running down the long road that winds through the darkening fir woods like an outsize rabbit seized with sudden domestic anxiety.

BESIDE THE BLUE MOUNTAINS

THE eerie character of the Grampians, their gloom and the sense of impending danger that dwells in their corries, is absent in the heights and folds of the Cairngorm range. If the Grampians whisper with terrifying secrecy, the Cairngorms sing strange songs of remoteness. It may seem absurd to speak so of hills, but those who have stepped among the high places are aware of such influences, though these matters are by no means easy to define in words.

Even from the plain, the Cairngorms dominate the mind. They are the only dreams that have ever stood still. It is impossible to wander through the forests, catching sight of the sudden snow-patterns of the heights among the black emphasis of branches, or to step the open road in view of that ranged majesty, without feeling continually drawn towards the hills, especially to the insistent passage of the Lairig Ghru. The shadow of its deep cut entices like a rent in the curtain of mystery, and at its entrance stands the green pyramid of the Eilrig which used to be a sanctuary for the deer. Mr. Seton Gordon gives the derivation of the name as " Eilercg, a V-shaped defile used as a deer-trap, probably referring to the neighbouring gully."[1] " Eileir " is the Gaelic for " a deer's walk " or " a sequestered

[1] *The Cairngorm Hills of Scotland*, Seton Gordon.

region," and one could wish that both the word and the pact had been preserved.

Out of the comfort of the forest into the magic of the Lairig, one's mind readjusts itself to the big scale of the scenery and undetailed vastness of the sweeping heights. The high hill-country is indeed not easily cast into individualities. Map and compass are sometimes necessities, but I have never yet met the hill-lover who could use them without feeling like an angel referring to Baedeker in Heaven. The last time I tried to orientate a map—I cannot say where it was, because I never found out—it was as if some demon resented my effort. I opened the map under what was momentarily the lee side of a big rock, and before it was fully unfolded it disappeared right out of my hand. There was not even a sound at its departure! Having carefully scrutinised the surrounding heather, I glanced up, and there was the puny representation of this mighty world, suspended in the mid air of the corrie, soaring about like a demented eagle. It landed in a stream and floated bobbing among young waterfalls and waltzing in little whirlpools in a manner most indecorous considering its scientific origin. When I achieved the rescue, the map was in two parts— a little tail of butter-muslin and a discoloured piece of paper ready to melt at a glance; the price of going for a ride with the Devil.

To pass from light allusion to serious illusion, one must admit that when such men as Dr. Kellas and Dr. Norman Collie, a Professor of Organic Chemistry, speak of encounters with a Supernatural Being in the Cairngorms, it is proof that such presences are not solely due to the imaginations of the hysterical and the ignorant.

Dr. Collie, in 1925, relating an early experience, said that he was climbing alone on the top of Ben MacDhui and was returning from the cairn in a mist when he began to think he heard some other things than merely the noise of his own footsteps in the snow. For every few steps he took he heard a big "crunch," and then another "crunch," as if some one was walking after him, but taking steps three or four times the length of his own. He said to himself, "This is all nonsense." He listened and heard it again, but could see nothing in the mist. As he walked on and the eerie "crunch, crunch" sounded behind him, he was seized with the most tremendous terror. Why, he did not know, for he did not mind being alone in the hills; but the uncanny "something" which he sensed caused fear to seize him by the throat. He took to his heels and ran staggering blindly among the boulders for four or five miles, nearly down to Rothiemurchus Forest.

Dr. Kellas saw a man come up out of the Lairig Ghru and wander round the cairn, near which his brother was sitting. What surprised him was that the man was practically the same height as the cairn, which was at least ten feet high, and he knew that it was not an ordinary thing for people to wander alone on the top of Ben MacDhui at midnight. The man descended to the Lairig. When Dr. Kellas asked his brother, "What on earth was that man doing walking round the cairn?" the brother replied, "I never saw any man at all."

At the time of my own experience I had not heard either of these reports. It was on a dull day, with light snow lying, and I had no further intention than to wander to the mouth of the Lairig, as walking was extremely difficult on the uneven and half-hidden surface.

Tired of the necessary concentration on the path, I stopped to enjoy the surroundings, the uprush of the cliffs of Creag a' Leth-choin, too steep to hold the snow, and the shadowed side of Sron na Lairig, and as I turned to retrace my steps I heard a voice of gigantic resonance. It spoke with the harsh consonants and full vowels of the Gaelic, but it issued so close to me that I was too startled, and I suppose I might as well confess, too scared, to unravel or even remember the sound of the words.

After the first momentary amazement, I tried to convince myself that it must be the echo of a deer's cry, but it came again close at hand from the very ground beneath my eyes; and leaving every margin for echoes or animal cries, it was impossible to convince myself that it was not human speech.

The only explanation I could summon was the possibility that some one might be lying hurt and unseen under the thin coat of snow, and the voice might be enlarged by unusual weather conditions. So I tramped in ever-widening circles until I had made sure that by retracing my steps towards the comfort of human habitation I was not deserting any one in distress. I was terribly anxious to get away, and as with Professor Collie, the gigantic footsteps followed me where no sound had been before. I was conscious of a strange feeling as if something walked right at my heel, but I was collected enough to count the seconds between the steps and realise that by their intervals they could not be echoes. It was at that moment of realisation, when the full knowledge came to me that the crunch and the little squeak of pressed snow did not tally with my own progress, that I forgot the risks of broken ankles, forgot all rules of common sense; blind to the surroundings, keeping to the path more by instinct than observation, I ran and stumbled till the wholesome sound of a dog barking somewhere about Whitewells dragged my mind free from a world of impossibilities to the realisation of normal humanity.

John Burton, a native of Deeside, writing in 1864, mentions the belief among the people of his own day that a ferocious giant patrolled the Pass, waving a fir tree in his hand. He had the power of diminishing his body and enlarging his head, and in such guise was given the name of Fahm.

Though James Hogg used the same spelling in boasting that he was acquainted with a man who had seen such a figure, there is really no such word. The name is undoubtedly Famh, as is further proven by the noun " Famhair," a giant. The name Famh is also the Gaelic for a mole, and Famhair stands equally for a giant or a mole-catcher. With these facts in mind, it is not so surprising to find that a supernatural mole, the size of a large dog, was also said to haunt the glens of the Monadh Ruadh, having a very large head compared to the size of its body.

So the giant and the mole are intermingled in the imagination, and for this there is excuse. The giant lives inside the hills, it is he who threw up the mountains in sport.   The mole, the little giant of the mysterious underworld, creates miniature hills. " Mountains out of mole-hills," in fact !   The unnatural mole was a destructive creature, leaving a slime on the grass which rendered the turf poisonous to horses.

Sir Thomas Dick Lauder does not mention the mole, but he suggests the natural phenomenon of the Brocken as a possible explanation of the giant Spectre.   A good idea ; but the enlarged shadow, thrown on a bank of mist, could not account for the sound of footsteps, nor can it be applied to a figure prowling in the black of night round a stationary object.   If the noise was confined to one particular area it would be only sensible to conclude that it was caused by echo, but even an echo cannot play a changing rhythm to a measured tread.

Perhaps he is related to the Urisk of the West who is described as " A large lubberly supernatural, of solitary habits and harmless character, that haunted lonely and mountainous places.   Having his dwelling in solitary and remote localities.   There were male and female Urisks, and the race was said to be the offspring of unions between mortals and faeries, that is, of the Lennan Sith.   The Urisk was usually seen in the evening, big and grey, sitting on the top of a rock and peering at intruders.   The wayfarer whose path led along the mountain-side, or along some desert moor, and who hurried for the fast-approaching nightfall, saw the Urisk sitting motionless on the top of a rock or slowly moving out of his way.   It spoke to some people and is even said to have thrashed them, but usually it did not meddle with the passer-by. On the contrary, it at times gave safe convoy to those who were belated." [1]

After all the evidence that can be gathered, we are no nearer a reasonable solution of the identity of the huge being who is felt, seen, and heard by persons of such widely different proclivities in the same vicinity. Are such things the concretion of the imaginings of the race, clinging to a particular place, discernible only to those whose racial sensitiveness is open to receive the primal impressions and fears of a bygone day? Or is the day not bygone? Even if the Urisk has become civilised as a Highland gentleman, what is he, this spirit that scales the summit of Ben MacDhui at midnight and roams the Lairig Ghru?

Among the foot-hills are the tales of mortal man; but the greater heights are sacred to the supernatural, to the deer, and the ptarmigan that skim the silence of the winter snows like souls in flight. The name ptarmigan in Sutherland also stands for butterfly, and butterflies in Celtic tradition are the souls of the dead, so that it is no wonder that every writer finds the same simile for the white birds of the snow.

The beauties of the Monadh Ruadh have been so successfully sung, their corries photographed, and their tracks set forth, that I will leave Ben MacDhui in its majesty and Loch A'an in its loneliness and all the giant's castles of rock and the boulder-fields awaiting their fate till the National Park Committee have come to a decision.

[1] *Superstitions of the Highlands and Islands*, J. G. Campbell.

The man who met one of the London Scottish just after a route-march with full kit through the Lairig, and asked him what he thought of the Cairngorms as a National Park, certainly got an answer in full. What it was full of one may guess. At any rate, the soldier did not seem to share my fear that the route would become popular !

The most accessible, and except for Loch A'an, the most impressive loch of the Monadh Ruadh is Loch Eanaich. The track to it is good enough to be cycled a little of the way; running first among the silence of the firs and up to the turn of the river, where the charm of " just round the corner " is so insistent that miles are magically lost, but where also a moment's distraction from the ruts, the rocks, the sand-heaps and boulders that strew the narrow track may land you into the cascading river below, beside the ancient pine, sole surviving warrior of the onslaughts of time and tempest.

At the opening of the actual glen, the twisting path runs across sudden bridges and the glacier hummocks which lie like small dumps of green dough left over from the sculptural work of the larger hills, and guard the way into the cul-de-sac. I suppose it is an instinct not to walk readily into a " pocket," and perhaps it is the mastering of that cautious feeling that adds to the thrill as the hills close down to the long bowl of the loch.

All before it, a bog of wicked blackness smears its ooze, cut into strange designs by the naked whiteness of decayed tree roots—the only sign that ever a tree has grown for miles around.

Some lochs have " safe " floors, suggestive of

covered meadows; others, like Loch Eanaich, are sudden, fathomless defiles from which the mountains rise in dizzy acuteness, giving a sense of depth interrupted only by a thin sheet of black glass. Round the southern precipice of this bowl even a sheep cannot find foothold; nothing but the silver tassels of the streams overhang the dark edge. To the side, far up on the slopes of Braeriach, the waters of Coire an Lochan lie, as if the Bodach had filled it as a goblet from the waters of the larger loch, and with raised elbow had forgotten to quaff the draught.

The Bodach is the spirit of the mountain that borders Loch Eanaich on the left side looking up towards the waterfalls. He quarrelled with the Cailleach standing opposite, and so great is their hatred that if The Old Man takes a fancy to you, The Woman will growl her dislike, but if she should feel favourable to you, The Man will voice his enmity.

The word Bodach literally means " old man," but used with the forces of Nature it bears reference to the supernatural, as Old Man Fox in the American folk-tales refers to something abnormal in the animal world.

Many hills in Scotland bear the name Bodach or Cailleach. The Old Woman is connected with a variety of affairs, such as the making of Loch Ness and many islands, and to her also was often attributed the fulness of corn and sea-wrack harvest. Not the sunny Ceres of the South, but a goddess as capricious as the climate; a Woman at whose least anger the sea boils, whose voice is the wind, whose abode is in the biggest mountains.

There were two stones representing The Old

Man and The Old Woman on the two hills of Loch Eanaich, and when, some years ago, one of them slid down on a small avalanche, there was something of apprehension in many a Speyside home.

They had neither of them indicated dislike or pleasure so far as my visits were concerned, until one day, as I stood beside the sluice-gates, the wind began to rise. It sounded at first no more than a full-chested sigh that disturbed the dipper on the white sand of the northern shore. Then little waves began to dance on the loch. The sun went in and ragged clouds began to scurry across the narrow sky, and a sudden small hurricane was accompanied by a conglomeration of weird sounds—giant laughter and sobs, interspersed with long eerie howls ! The wind was playing on the crevices of the Bodach's scaurs, roaring up the rock chimneys and escaping with screams, hitting slabs of rock with noise like a blast and whistling down ravines to echo on the surface of the water.

I did not wait to hear whether a change of wind would give the same effect from the opposite hill, because a lash of hail, followed by a faint rumble of thunder, sent me on the run to the lower bothy. To face a storm alone in the mountains is an experience one does not easily forget or readily repeat. The thunder is incessant, echoing from hill to hill as if the bens themselves were disintegrating, and the lightning either arrows into every crevice, especially the one you are sheltering in, or seems to malignantly trickle its fire down the slopes to your very feet. So it was with a feeling that I could do with some comfort on the matter that I appealed to

LOCH INSH

(page 49)

Donald, asking him to reassure me that there was some safety in my plan of lying flat in the heather on such harrowing occasions. I knew that he had been alone in a remote glen during one of the worst storms ever known in the district.

" The best thing to do in a thunderstorm in the hills? " he repeated, looking into the distance with his weatherwise eyes, and considering the importance of his reply.

" Well, I 'll tell you what I always do myself. I 'll surely tell you the best thing to do in the hills— a bad place to be in a storm. The best thing to do is just to take no notice of it, no notice of it whatever."

Useful advice to one whose very shin-bones go soft, whose heart behaves like a tent-flap in the wind at the first distant growl! Not that it is always the rowdy things either among humanity or the elements that are the most dangerous, and Glen Eanaich was the scene of a silent tragedy in the days of timber-floating.

Early in the spring, a widow's only son went up the glen in the dark of morning to raise the sluice-gates and release the water to float the logs that were waiting many miles down the bed of the dammed stream.

The arrival of the volume of water was a sure signal that he had trudged the eleven miles from his home in safety and opened the gates, and not till late afternoon was it realised that he had not returned. Those who went up to the loch to search, found him sitting beside the sluice-gates, dead, with his half-eaten breakfast in his hand. He had sat down to rest and take his food, and, numbed by the cold, had dozed. While he slept, the incredibly soft plaid of a local snowstorm had covered his Grant tartan and deepened his sleep beyond waking.

There are two bothies in the glen—both originally the gift of a Grant who was born near the loch at the time of the spring pasturing, when his mother, the wife of the Laird of Rothiemurchus, had accompanied her tenants to the peaceful spot. He stipulated that free food and shelter were always to be provided in each bothy; but be warned—hungry wrath would be the only result of trusting to tradition in this case.

If you turn to the right after the lower bothy as you come up the glen, a path will take you to Loch Mhic Gille Chaoile, the loch of the thin or swift man's son, who added bravery to his inherited fleetness. Up beside this loch, the Herd or Bowman of Rothiemurchus was alone guarding the cattle on the Sabbath day, when he heard distant yet unmistakable sounds of raiders from Lochaber. Wasting no time, he dropped into the shelter of the larger glen and ran to the Church, where he knew the people would be assembled. There the service ended abruptly at his breathless news. Every man was to the door, his hand on his dirk, but the fleetest of them all was the Son of the Thin Man. He was away among the firs of the forest before his comrades were well clear of the fields; up among the heather before they had left the shadow of the forest, past the sithean, over the shoulder of the hill and beside the loch before the others were near for his assistance, but not before the caterans were busy rounding up the cattle. Perhaps it would have been no more than common sense to hide, and reasonable caution to have followed the robbers unperceived, but lochs of the hills are not named after the cautious, and the exhibitors of common sense do not have their names handed down through the firelight of years.

The Thin Man's Son did his best against some twenty armed men, and was then killed and buried before his helpers came on the scene! The raiders were chased away and the cattle retrieved with no other loss of life, but the whereabouts of the body of the fleet-footed one remained a mystery.

Some weeks later, a woman journeying from Lochaber told of his death and passed word of the burial-place, and the grateful folks of Rothiemurchus found his remains and buried them in their own churchyard.[1] Mr. Seton Gordon mentions in connection with the tale that a dagger was found near the loch to confirm the narrative.

To this hero, whose name in the old Gaelic tales meant " a sword," has been attributed the hidden treasure of Rothiemurchus, which is to be found " where the White Serpent goes into the hole."

Has any one looked in the Slochd of Bachdcharn in Abernethy where the White Serpent of healing lived, or under the loch at Balliefurth which was guarded by a monster? Or even searched behind the meaning of these mythologic words?

[1] *The Cairngorm Hills of Scotland*, p. 153, Seton Gordon.

KINGUSSIE

In the year 1371, King Robert II. bestowed the lands and lordship of Badenoch on his son Alexander. The Court's loss was no gain to the northern district, and the first polite appellation of the Highlanders, " Alasdair Mor Mac an Righ," soon gave place to the more truthfully descriptive nickname of " The Wolf of Badenoch."

Savage even beyond the roughness of his time, and of ungovernable temper, Alexander ranged his lands, spreading terror before him. He established himself securely by rebuilding the castles of Ruthven at Kingussie, Loch an Eilein in Rothiemurchus, and Loch an Dorb in the North. From them he pursued his feuds against the Bishop of Moray, without consideration for the innocent peasantry, burning their houses and seizing their cattle to feed his soldiers while he avenged the censure of the Church upon his partnership with the Lady Mariota Athyn.

This lady's domestic life can hardly have come under the heading of a Joyous Adventure with such an ill-tempered lord, and yet his fierce affection was genuine and he brooked no hint against the mother of his five sons, even though his legal wife was the Countess of Ross.

The interference of the Church on the subject roused the Wolf's anger beyond bounds, and in revenge he destroyed all the ecclesiastical buildings of both Forres and Elgin. Such wanton destruction seems incredible in a man brought up at Court, but since he *was* so constituted, his death at least should have been in the nature of a Grande Finale. It does not seem a fit ending for a man of flaming savagery that he should have done penance in Perth, walking barefoot to show his repentance before entering the Monastery at Haddington. There he spent his last days, writing out his sins like a child with a copy-book, and died in the quiet company of book and candle, to be buried in the Cathedral of Dunkeld.

It is surely a privilege divided between the humbug and the certified Saint to " rejoice " over a sinner that repents, and the crowds that lined the streets of the Fair City to see the Wolf forswear his manhood must have felt the shame of his act and preferred to have witnessed his death. Alasdair the Big could just as well have vented his mighty wrath " against " evil as " for " it. Strong arms were needed in his day and in his district under the complicated land-system of baronies and davochs, and one indomitable character could have welded the Clans into a body with one aim, instead of encouraging every sort of lawlessness. Badenoch was no mean heritage. At one time it included not only, as now, Laggan, Kingussie, Insh, and Alvie, but also Rothiemurchus, Kincardine, Duthil, Garten, and even Inverlaidon. It was feued to various Clans, who, of course, had individual aspirations as soon as their strength permitted.

In the thirteenth century the Comyns held Badenoch, and no one but the Wolf who succeeded them

had a more cruel hold over the people. When the
Wolf took to the Cloister, he left no legitimate heir,
though his eldest son, the Earl of Mar, may have
replaced him for a short time. If the son ruled, he
left no mark of improved conditions, having inherited the less endearing qualities of his sire, as may
be judged from the fact that he enforced his wooing
with the help of a band of caterans, who were probably the companions of his younger brother. It
was altogether a good day for Kingussie when
James II. gave the lordship to the Earl of Huntly.
Then the Priory rose, and men of learning came to
Cean Ghiubhsaiche (the Head of the Fir Wood),
advertising by their undisturbed contentment the
pleasures of a peaceful life. This influence was
somewhat counteracted by the building of a new
Castle on the ruins of the Wolf's stronghold of
Ruthven. It was an edifice significant of the new
power, a challenge that was not overlooked by
Argyll, who besieged it vigorously but without avail.

Like the man who pleaded guilty to having
broken another's nose, giving as sufficient provoca-
tion that it " protruded," so the surrounding Chiefs
looked on Ruthven. It roused a warlike spirit on
all sides and was the scene of many a small fray,
besides being captured in turn by Leslie and
MacKenzie of Pluscarden and finally utterly de-
molished by Claverhouse.

The year 1718 saw Government barracks rising
over the shattered remains. A great square fort,
its main building formed a square surrounding a
courtyard; and from the interior no view was
obtainable of the beauty of the strath stretching

unbroken to the wooded Tor of Alvie, because only narrow gun-slots broke the blank uprising of the outer walls. In the courtyard, slab-stairs led to the soldiers' apartments and to the upper gun-parapet. A guard-room abutted at one corner, the kitchen at another, and an enclosing wall ran round the entire mound. The stables, with outer stairs leading to lofts above, stood separately. Two companies of soldiery could be housed in this impregnable fortress, and the men who joined Cope on his march to Inverness in 1745 were stationed in Ruthven. They left only one sergeant and ten men on guard when they proceeded North, and can hardly have been surprised to hear the news that the little band had been attacked. That these few redcoats managed to repulse an attacking force of 200 seems almost unbelievable, but of what use were dirks, swords, or bullets against thick stone walls?

There must have been some chink, some weak spot known to the enemy, for a year later a repetition attack on the same company, even though the defending party was larger, ended in the defeat of the Government men. The attackers were the fugitives from Culloden, who, with their fighting spirit still aflame, made the Castle a rallying-ground till a message from Prince Charles Edward bade them disperse.

Then it was that all that was burnable of Ruthven rose in flames, lighting the strath from end to end. A colour ruddier than the scarlet of redcoats filled the great square as the fire roared and crackled, shooting up like gigantic flags of defiance when the heavy timbers crashed from the roof. Though it was an empty revenge, there must have been a little satisfaction in the distressed hearts of the beaten men as they saw the devouring tongues lick the gun-slots which should never again support the death-dealing muskets of the enemy, and watched the sparks like tears of fire melt into the swamp below.

The shell still stands, but now nettle and thistle guard its walls and the wind whistles through the wide cracks that rive from ground to gable. Stables without horses, guard-rooms without men, strong walls without a roof—Ruthven is no more than a monster firegrate, where high dreams and brave hopes went up in smoke.

Apart from the Castle, Kingussie fills me with a longing for something unusually elegant and efficient in the shape of a pickaxe. A scratch here, a dig there, might reveal so much, for Kingussie sits heavily on its past. One old kirkyard is strewn with rubbish, and bits of old walls are to be found joined to modern houses as if some ancient building were trying to escape from under an oppressor. The ground feels as if it is compressed upon things which cry out for the daylight. The silver mine is turfed over; the Roman camp, left from the invasion of Agricola, is now hardly discernible; and the old Cladh up by the Smiddy is knee-deep in grass.

In this quiet place the tombstones of MacKintosh and Cameron stand aslant. Stray hens find their way through the rusty gate to lay the symbol of life among the damp dead. The weeds are not even downtrodden as a guiding path to the monument that marks the site of the Chapel personally founded by St. Columba. The sacred stone is set in the wall, the base of it formed from a Holy Water Stoup (the compromise of Christianity from the use of dew-cups), and the ivy that sprawls over the four walls of the enclosure clusters in overhanging thickness round the arch.

Here on a day in June the lush grass sighed lazily

ST. COLUMBA'S STONE, KINGUSSIE

and the gnats danced in silent ecstasy. The dark privacy of the heavy creeper contrasted with the unhindered sprays of wild rose that shed payment of petals among the graves that fostered their roots; and when a lark rose from its hidden nest beside a broken rail, it might well have been the spirit of some singing lass suddenly released to tell her tale of exuberant joy.

It was to an Inn at Kingussie that I came one night, soaked to the skin. My very pockets were full of water, but the hostess seemed not to notice the streams that my advent created on her speckless floor, and her welcome was almost warm enough to dry one's clothes on the spot. I had to remove my pack before I could negotiate the narrow corridors, the floors of which were as undulating as the tracks I had been treading. I tripped on a sudden step up, and missed my breath as another took me down in contradiction, and out of a tiny green-glass window I stared at an unbelievable moon. A moon so distorted as to resemble a Catherine-wheel. To add to the strange effect, the sound of the old Gaelic songs robustly sung rumbled up from some lower region, as if the foundations were voicing their sentiments. It was a house where one could easily lose oneself, not only among the bends of passages, but among the twists of Time, and I passed a day of blended physical comfort and mental enchantment before I passed from its shelter with the Gaelic blessing on my journeying.

Kingussie is at its liveliest at the time of the sheep-dog trials. Then farmer and shepherd, kilted laird and leather-coated lady, wend their way among dogs and cars up the road beside the many waterfalls.

On that day, even the Station, which normally has the appearance of having contentedly shuffled away to dream, wears an air of alertness and resounds to the banging of carriage doors, the competitive whistling of engine and shepherd, the low growling of dogs, and the sound of tackety boots on the iron steps.

By eight in the morning the 'buses have disgorged their packed masses, and the shepherds, usually the first on the field, are eyeing the course. Eager onlookers spread themselves on the hillside to begin that insidious sliding which is unnoticeable as actual movement, but which mysteriously and insistently lands the sturdy boots of the more elevated spectators into the necks of those lower down the slope.

As for the Judges—whatever they may be in private life, they take on for the day the importance and exclusiveness of kings. They pass the hours hidden in tents that face the course, widely roped off from the ordinary people, who can only observe from occasional shadows and from bulgings on the canvas that judgment is being passed.

The sturdy kilts of the local Lairds enrich the scene early in the day, but the queer kilts come later, flapping like thin flannel above knees that belie the tartan.

For all the uncanny understanding of the dogs, never is the gap between man and beast so pathetically exhibited. The three foolish sheep are brought down the fairway, trotting stupidly with the non-plussed expression of a platform party that has not been allocated seats. In spite of being a " mixed " flock they are herded and penned with a fusion of patience and guile; but when, having " shed " one sheep, the dog is told to add it again, his whole body expresses surprise at such sudden aberration in a man whose character he thought he knew. To be called off a half-finished job because " time is up " is a matter beyond explanation, though the Master tries to fondle away the strained expression that asks, " What 's amiss? Have I done wrong? Am I in disgrace? Mayn't I round them off?" The very thinness of the wall that divides animal from human understanding is a tragedy, and it hurts to see a shepherd lad on his knees with his arms round a glossy coat, giving and pleading but not able to exchange youthful confidences.

In the Open Stakes at Kingussie, " Jets " and Hemps " of Derbyshire run against " Sheilas " of Ireland and Scottish dogs from the four quarters; and in the afternoon when the tea-urn begins to boil and corks to pop, there arises such a conglomeration of dialects that one supposes each man to be arguing with himself, for who else could comprehend him?

Then, too, there is time to glance behind at the brown uplands where Loch Gynach lies hidden; and down to where, behind the darkness of the fir woods, the Spey winds widely on its way. Ruthven looks less blind from the height, and its mound preserves throughout the year an enamel green that shames the first larches of spring.

On such a night the village looks more as it must have done in the days of the Pitmain Tryst. The Tryst was the yearly cattle sale, and dinners and dancing and bargaining and tale-telling were so combined that for one night at least the home-goer would be full of courage and ready to defy the two Witches themselves. The Witch of Laggan, though far distant, was not unknown as a visitor at Kingussie, though the village did not need her services, for it had a witch of its own who lived at the foot of a hillock to the north of the town. Her cottage has been burnt, but the knoll on which she performed her awful rites still stands beside the road, and is now topped by the War Memorial.

It is not easy to direct strangers to the Cave of Raitts, for it has no landmark near it, no path to it, no trees behind it, and indeed you could stand within five yards of its gaping entry unaware. It is not possible to indicate its exact whereabouts in an official manner. To such places one must take a friend by the arm, and, standing by the last cottage in Lynchat facing Kingussie, walk to the first gate on the right which leads along a fence dividing a field. The fence is the guide to the edge of a wood, and then the wood is guide to the top of the hill. When almost at the summit, a right angle across the field brings you to a six-foot hole that drops into the burrow known as " The Cave of Raitts," marked incorrectly on most maps as a Pictish House.

The word Raitt is a form of the Irish " rath "— a dwelling inside a hill, which later came to be applied mostly to faerie knolls. The present " dwelling " is an excavation of horse-shoe shape, lined with boulders and roofed with great slabs of stone which are overgrown with turf. If the cave is hard to find now, it must have been a wonderful hiding-place in the days when the roof was complete, leaving as the only entry a hole about three feet square at one end of the curve.

Tradition has it that the MacNivens built the cave the better to slaughter the cattle of the Mac-Phersons, to whom revenge was due for some now forgotten deed. A cottage was built on top of the hill, and was inhabited by two females who helped by their repulsive appearance to keep that quarter isolated.

One evening a beggar was found at the door of the cottage in a state of collapse. He was dying, he said, from Galar-fuail and he pleaded for shelter. The two women may have been ill to look upon, but they were too kind-hearted to turn the invalid away, and bringing him in, set the guest before the fire, nor bothered to notice whether or not he watched them as they went about their usual duties of redding the room and putting the food into the cupboard. They fed him and bade him good-night, leaving him to sleep beside the fire.

As the first grey light of dawn changed the space of the window from black to silver and the cold morning wind found its way into the cottage, the beggar awoke and felt hungry. His hostesses still snored in the inner room, so he decided to help himself to the round of cold beef which he had seen placed in the cupboard along with other food. He rose quietly and opened the press door. There was no beef, no meal, no milk! Of the viands and vessels which had been placed there the night before, not a trace remained; moreover, half the cupboard floor was agape, and by cautiously inserting his head the beggar could hear the sound of gruff voices issuing as if from the grave.

He crept back to his sleeping-place, and later, after thanking his hostesses, limped painfully away down the hillside. Once clear of possible observation, he took to his heels in robust style and was soon telling the successful results of his espionage to the impatient MacPhersons.

The MacPhersons' revenge was very complete, but the Clan to whom the pretended invalid belonged is still said to suffer from his assumed complaint.

A later gang, not of respectable cattle reivers, but of common robbers, inhabited the cave in 1773, but they lost enjoyment in the ploy after their leaders were hanged in Inverness.

If the MacNivens were the constructors of the cave, then I cannot honestly greatly grieve at the tale of their rout; because it is obvious that the stupendous granite slabs that serve for roofing, most of them nearly six feet in length, are the original "Standard stanys de la Rathe de Kyngucy," a ring which must have been one of the biggest and most important stone circles in Badenoch or on Speyside. That it was used as a mote or judgment place is known, as the Wolf of Badenoch held his Court within the circle in 1380 for the Bishop of Moray to show his titles of land tenure. The Bishop, disagreeing as to the authority of his Lordship, refused to stand "within the circle," and "without the circle" was unofficial ground where an oath was not necessarily binding.

Beyond the wood lay the Castle of Raitts, whose dungeons are now the cellars of Balavil House, and which was the scene of a famous banquet held by the Comyns. They were Lords of Badenoch at the time, but were constantly threatened by the growing power of the MacKintoshes. Indeed, a small fight showed all too plainly for the Comyns which way the wind blew, and they thought it wise to sue for peace, and invited the MacKintoshes to a feast as an indication of goodwill.

The guests were to be seated alternately with the Comyns, and at a given signal every Comyn was to raise his sgian dubh and carve the MacKintosh at his right-hand side, and that would be that. The guests came and took their places as required, making good among the viands and ale, while the Comyns kept a covert eye upon their Chief as they waited for the tragic signal; but the MacKintosh, having overheard a whispered word, gave a signal first, and the Comyns (the left-hand neighbour of every guest) felt the sudden scorching drive of steel and remained silent when the enemy rose from the table with the gesture of "Shall we join the ladies?"

On this spot, saturated with ancient tale and serene with the beauty of hill and forest, lived James MacPherson, famed for his Ossianic poems. His estate claimed some of the loveliest timber in this land of towering trees. MacPherson himself planted fir and larch and elm and birch, which still stand, a far more fitting memorial to the man who sang of the moon lost in the heavens, who loved the broken clouds and stream and wind, than the tomb he coveted and won in Westminster Abbey.

LOCH AN EILEIN

(page 79)

KINCRAIG

From Kingussie to Kincraig is just a natural step along the King's Highway, but if ever any place might be described as "two-faced," it is Kincraig.

If you come upon it from Alvie or Kingussie, you find a modern village with a big Post Office and an uninteresting station, the whole with the atmosphere of a deserted Church Hall; but if you come by the road that winds on the other side of the river, dropping from the hills on to the flat shore of Loch Insh where the tide rides like a sea over the machair, you will find two humped peninsulas with crowns of pine, and on one of them a tiny white Church perched like a nesting gull.

If you would start at "the beginning," go up the serpentine track that marks it as a place of Druidic worship before the Christian occupation of the seventh century. There, sitting on some of the exposed tree roots, you may look upon the same scene as those white-robed mystics viewed some thousands of years ago. To be sure, the knoll was an island then, but so it often is to the present day when melting snows overfill the river. The long vista of Loch Insh is undisturbed right up to the place where, as the MacFarlane MS. expresses it, " the river de-boggeth into the Loch." The mountains, too distant to be reflected, gain in dignity by the long and undetailed foreground; and though in the days of Druid and Culdee they were clothed almost to the summits with trees, the Little Black Hill still sits at the feet of the Yellow Mountain, and the rise that hides the burial of an unknown Scandinavian King stares resignedly into the future from above the bonny woods of Dunachton, which is said to be the fort of Nectan, King of the Picts.

In this spot of all places in Scotland one should hear the rustle of phantom Druid robes. So direct is the association it almost takes one's breath away, for—not more than forty-eight years ago—the last representative of the Druidic Priestesses died in this district! I wish I could have heard the old lady giving orders that she was to be buried in the white dress which she had worn each year at the Féill Colmcille.

The Fair was also the yearly market where pedlar and packman, wrestler and songster, gathered to make the most of an otherwise religious festival, held in their day to the honour of St. Columba, though probably of far older origin. There is reason for the connection with St. Columba, even though the date of the Fair coincided with a Druidic festival, for the Church on the knoll was founded by Adamnan; but it is most improbable that either the Saint or his disciple instituted the rule that the women of Insh should wear white dresses for the occasion.

The uniform is a recognition of office, and St. Columba did not encourage women in the ministry; far from doing so, he regarded them with averted glance; there was no suggestion of a Nunnery on Iona in his day.

The Druids did include women in their orgies and

retained authorised Priestesses on the islands of Sena and Anglesea, who were connected with an even older cult which included nine muse-like maidens who fanned the flames below Keridwen's cauldron of Inspiration.[1]

If these white-robed Priestesses were also installed on the island of Insh, the succeeding Culdee or Christian would find it easier to convert than to oust them. St. Columba himself retained some of the Druidic rites. He is said to have buried his disciple Oran alive as a sacrifice to the island of Iona, and on finding the victim still living when uncovered on the third day and able to say that "Death is no wonder, nor is Hell as it is said," St. Columba cried, "Tuilleadh uir air Odhran," which is still used as an equivalent to the rather impolite expression "Shut up." There are certainly rites and ceremonies joining the two faiths like knots in a thread, a thread that stretches from the remote past of Celtic mysticism into the early nineteenth century at Insh.

I once spent a whole day on the mound, from the first streak of early daylight till night drew blue curtains round its pebbly shore. Such a tiny world it is to contain so many treasures besides the flowers that grace its central meadow. Under the root of a tree I found an owl's nest, lined with down so soft that one could see but hardly feel it; an egg as round as a billiard ball lay snugly in its midst.

The island also had its mystery murder, for there was no sign of hurt on the newly dead magpie that lay on its side with one pied wing outstretched. It

---

[1] See *The Mysteries of Britain*, Lewis Spence.

was impossible not to feel saddened by the droop of its silken head, yet there is an air of masquerade about the pyot, as if a faerie prince had borrowed the sombre garb of the clergy, black gloves and all, but the gaiety of his green and blue satin peeps through the disguise.

It used to be considered a most unlucky deed to kill this bird, because it harbours a drop of the Devil's blood on its tongue. With the same thought the Italians call it " Gazza," a divulger of secrets, from which we took the word gazette. As a bringer of bad luck it is no longer potent one would judge, since every gamekeeper's vermin rack is bedecked with the lovely plumage, for the eggs of grouse, though a dainty dish, are not for such as he.

Four swans shared my midday meal; they were beautiful as ships upon the calm of the waters, but by no means gentle in their manners, indeed their masterfulness rather demanded than requested my sandwiches, and I divided my admiration of their snowy plumage with apprehension of their superior demeanour. Not that I had any right to resentment, since they are the real proprietors of the island. The Church is built upon the site of the Chapel of the Swans, containing as its greatest treasure an early Celtic bell which sang as it flew.

The swans were leisurely pluming themselves, sometimes glancing up at me with an almost human and most humorous expression in their round black eyes. Some instance, half-remembered, stirred my thoughts as the water was stirred by their restless feet. A monk—a Celtic bell—swans—a Chapel. Then suddenly I knew—and not myself, but the

centuries that lie behind me, sang to the snowy
exiles,—sang their own story to—the Children of
Llyr.

Llyr, the green Sea God, father of Mannan who
hides yet among the mists of the Isle of Man, had
four children by his first wife. These three sons
and the daughter of the Sea, with limbs as white as
the foam and eyes dark as sea-deeps, were as loved
by their father as they were hated by their step-
mother; and the latter satisfied her evil desires by
turning them into swans. Nine hundred years was
the time of their wandering. From place to place
over the earth, wide white-winged they flew, singing
exquisitely. They were discovered on a little island
by a priest of St. Patrick, and with his quad-
rangular bell he summoned them to the Christian
altar. Day after day they answered the call of the
bronze bell and worshipped in the Chapel, joined
one to another by silver chains. When they were
taken to visit Deoch, wife of the King of Connacht,
they at last resumed their human shape. They
changed, yes; but from the winged energy and
beauty of swans they became shrivelled human
beings with the weight of nine hundred years upon
bowed backs. Before they died the Priest baptized
them. Died? Can the children of the Sea die?
Do the waves not still wash the shores of Tir-an-og,
and is the echo of them not heard upon the shores
of Insh?

The bell in the present Church may have called to
the swans, but it had other strange powers of its own.
It could fly through the air and sing as it went;
more than that, it possessed homing powers without

which it would no longer have been at Insh, for it was borrowed frequently for its healing properties, and just as frequently those who benefited from its services desired to retain it.

When this occurred, and Perth or Scone was the last town to be guilty, the bell returned of itself singing, "Tom an Eunan, Tom an Eunan." The site has been called the mound of Eunan as another

THE BELL OF INSH

name for Adamnan or a form of Iain, but in either case it stands for "The Bird One."

The Bell of St. Fillan is exactly similar in shape, and it too went on merciful visits to places, including Perth or Scone, and now rests on a little island among the waters of Loch Shiel. The other travelling bell was the Bell of St. Modan at Ardchattan, which Dr. Angus Smith connects with the island in the Loch of the Swans to the south. This Clag Buidhe, as it was named, could also heal and see itself safely home, singing sweetly on the way, and it too was borrowed by Scone. The first time it returned from there on its own power, but the second journey ended in disaster. "An rud nach buin duit, na buin da," "Don't meddle with that which meddles not with you," it sang on its homeward way and then went astray, lost in " some forgotten mere among the tumbled fragments of the hills." There were people living in the nineteenth century who claimed to have heard the music of this flying bell. Because these bells were all particularly efficacious for head troubles, we need not conclude that the neighbourhood of Perth was harbouring all the imbeciles of the land. At the time of the bell's best known exploits, Scone, where the stone of Destiny lay, was the very centre of Scottish civilisation.

The Bell of Insh is there to see and handle, but for every clang of its iron tongue bad luck falls on the ringer. Exactly like the Bell of St. Fillan, except that it has an unadorned handle, the Bell of Insh stands in an ancient stone cup which serves as a window-sill inside the Church. It is securely chained, which seems a mockery, but if there are still weak heads in Scotland, there are meddlers too, and the lost Clag Buidhe has never been found.

The Church on the site of the Chapel of the Swans is entered over ancient gravestones; the original door, long since blocked up, having faced south. The outside is pleasing in its simplicity. White walls and grey-lined windows, dove-coloured roof and open-swung bell; but inside the broken beauty of cobblestone floor and the central position of the pulpit have given way to covering boards, to conventional arrangement and an over-free use of varnish in an atmosphere of stove and duster that little accords with the reverence one naturally feels in a spot that has upheld spirit over matter for thousands of years.

Facing the two knolls lies one of the entrances to Invereshie House; a mansion screened by trees and backed by the roaring Feshie. Its first Laird, a MacPherson, succumbed to the charms of Miss Shaw of Dalnavert. He was not the first to discover the falsity of the statement that " two can live as cheaply as one," but indeed the lady went out of her way to display the open hand in spite of continual remonstrances from her husband. Thus she rapidly reduced the estate to comparative poverty, and altercations on the subject of expense were frequent and fierce.

One night, after an unusually angry scene, the lady decided to return to her father's house. It was inconvenient that her family lived on the other side of the Feshie, and that there was neither bridge nor boat to assist her passage; but such a drawback is just the feeble kind of impasse that does occur when one is determined to take some fury-driven step. While the lady stood on the brink of the river deliberating on the difficulty of her situation, her husband had taken a walk to cool his ire and arrived in the same neighbourhood. He realised that he stood on the verge of ruin, and was also deliberating his next move in a difficult situation. The lady came to a decision first, by trying to ford the Feshie, and was bowled over by the flood and swept towards the malignant Spey. She would certainly have been drowned but that the air in her four petticoats buoyed her up. "Ay," said old Jean, when last she repeated the story to me, " her *four* petticoats held her up," and she added with a swift glance of criticism at my attire, " Where would she have been but for them?" I suggested that maybe it was the expense of such profuse raiment that had been the last straw to the Laird's wrath, and that if she had not been so encumbered she might have won across. However, I had to admit that the Lady of Invereshie had good reason to be thankful for her skirts once she was afloat, as they kept her up until she was able to grasp a branch that overhung the water, and seeing at the same time the figure of her Guidman on the bank, she implored him to save her.

This point in the story Jean always illustrates with pleading gestures which employ both hands (leaving no reason why the lady in question should not have been swept away by the current), and she puts up a wavering prayer so intermixed between appeal to husband and Fate as to suggest that for the moment they might be one and the same. She waits panting for the all-important question, " What did Invereshie do?" The answer being that he " out " with his sgian dubh and severed the life-saving branch with the words, "You have already taken much from me, you may take that too."

Perhaps the look his wife gave him at the parting made him relent, perhaps he had carefully gauged the exact extent of his punishment; in either case he jumped into the Feshie and rescued her. "And," says Jean, "the Lady had a will of her own and so she looked up to him for his bit of heat, indeed she liked him the better for it, and they lived both amicably and economically so that the estate descended in good condition to their son Aeneas."

"Would you have liked a husband who would have let you half drown, Jean?" I asked her. "There's no such man as would dare do the like to me ever been born," she replied; whether with regret or pride I could not tell.

The daughter of Dalnavert would have had a fair step to go after she had crossed the Feshie, for her path home lay over the moor and past Loch Geal. The name means White Loch, and while up-to-date information gives it a white sand and clay ground, accounting for the wonderful clearness of the water, and cites it as being of great depth and purity, legend records it as bottomless and the haunt of hairy trout. And legend is right on the first point, for an underground tunnel must connect either with the Feshie or the Spey, as the waters of the loch, minus any visible outlet or inlet, rise and fall with great rapidity and have been known to overflow when the rivers were in spate.

As for the hairy fish, they swim between reality and legend in the most confusing manner. I met a fisher who had personally known some one who had caught just such a trout. He described it as having very thick scales, from each of which a fine hair, light in colour and about half an inch in length, protruded, giving the creature a most unnatural and revolting appearance.

Having but little faith in anglers' tales at second-hand, I sought the advice of one whose whole life has been spent near the loch. He told me that he had once found a dead fish there which had " very rough skin and very thick scales but no sign of hair." He remembers the old people of the district telling how trout had been " carried from the river Feshie in tubs and put in Loch Geal " when the river was flooded and many trout stranded in the pools among the islands. Though it sounds most probable that unusual depth of water in a still and unfed loch might be the cause of a parasitic disease, an eminent piscatologist has not been able to identify such a malady, and therefore suggests that the term might mockingly allude to very old cannibal trout. Perhaps in the old days, before trout from another source were introduced, there may have been some local disease caused by a particularly dry season when even the subterranean inlet would have been unable to feed the loch ; for there is nothing to give rise to the legend, unless it was a tale arranged by the secret distillers who used the advantage of the pure water for their illicit stills. The uninitiated would prefer to give wide berth to a lochan containing such an uncanny population, especially at dusk, and the good trade could continue without fear of molestation.

Have the hairy trout been guardians of the barley brew, or are they perhaps the result of it ; or was there at one time a disease, or is there some hidden connection with devil or ancient god which is indiscernible as Loch Geal's hidden outlet?

Beyond the loch lie peaceful meadow-lands, the last place for thoughts of conflict to assail the mind, yet, in the days when Napoleon menaced Britain, a small army gathered here to drill with pomp and diligence. The green background of this plain was the setting for kilt and plumed bonnet, and the Laird of Rothiemurchus as Lieutenant-Colonel was mounted on a charger, his saddle bedecked with goatskins and fine trappings. He was only outshone by his wife, who proudly accompanied him. Her costume consisted of " a tartan petticoat gaudily laced, a bonnet with feathers, further embellished by a large cairngorm." [1] Perhaps the place of drill was not unfitting ; for Dal na vert or Dail na bheart is given by Professor MacBain as meaning " The place of the graves," being the burial-place of the slain from the battle between the Scandinavian King Harold and Nectan. This derivation makes me wonder at the local pronunciation which accents the second syllable, and unaccountably stresses the preposition.

The estates of Dalnavert and South Kinrara were known as " The Davochs of the Head," being part of an unusual compensation. The Laird of MacKintosh, in an ill-advised moment, decided to attack Auchindoune Castle while its owner, the Earl of Huntly, was elsewhere. Having burnt the Castle to the ground, and with retribution at his heels, the offender made an effort to appeal to the Earl in person. It was unlucky for him that the Earl was away from home, and mercy proved no surer in a woman's hands, for the outraged Countess avowed that there should be no forgiveness till the transgressor's head was on the block. Was it genuine remorse or sudden blind anger that sent the MacKintosh down to the shadowed kitchen quarters

[1] *Memoirs of a Highland Lady*, Elizabeth Grant of Rothiemurchus.

to give a strange order to the cook? Many a sheep
and many a bullock had the man with the axe
tackled, but here was different killing! Perhaps
the MacKintosh did not expect the order to be
obeyed, or else anticipated interference before the
blow should be dealt, but the man did not hesitate
at the bloody deed. Could they tell from the expression of the severed head as it lay on the flagstone
floor in what mood this man had met death?

Huntly on his return felt acutely the unpardon-
able treatment of the guest, and gave South Kinrara
and Dalnavert to the dead man's successor.

From this tragic house with its wide pastures a
little footpath goes past the place called Mean or
Humble, and over a wooden bridge across the Spey
to the open Moor of Alvie, whose gravel cliffs seem
ever aslide into the hurrying waters of the river.

BY THE LILIES OF ST. AILBHE

THE evening air had a quality as of water, suggested perhaps by the green-blue tint in the height of the western sky. The rocky surface of An Sguabach, half a mile across the marsh, looked as though a finger-length would reach it. Not a breath stirred the cross-stitch patterns of the Lady's-straw at my feet or allowed wafted communication among the airy bluebells that made patterns of congealed atmosphere along the edge of the uncut hayfield. The loch, cleft with the little peninsula that holds the Church, was an unrippled sheet of silver foil, beyond which rose the comfortable and sheltering mound of the pine-covered Tor.

The sudden roar of an express train to Inverness was as distressing as an earthquake, but it passed in seconds, leaving a silence as sudden as its sweeping appearance, and nothing more fell into the quiet of Alvie. The place keeps its peace because both trains and cars pass on, leaving undisturbed the crofts, the woods, the open fields, the loch, and heather-covered hills. Alvie is fittingly named after a Saint, and its lily-girdled Church is still its centre.

St. Ailbhe first appears in the timelessness of myth, being the son of Olchu by his maidservant who ran away before her child was born. She was traced, however, by her lover's master, Cronan, who, like the god Cronus, seemed to have a dislike of bairns and ordered the babe to be thrown upon the hillside. The mother placed the child under the shelter of a rock from which he took his name " Ail," a rock, and Lochlan, son of the Strong One " Laidhir," found him being suckled by a wolf.

It would seem as if the Saint had little encouragement for his saintly behaviour, as not only did his father's name mean Evil, but his foster-father had married a lady of the same unpretentious name related to Olchu, the father of Ailbhe. The wolf's den was in Ireland, and not till we hear of Lochlan giving the waif to a British tribe in the vicinity does he become more tangible in the shape of a legendary character. The Britons baptized the boy and brought him to Britain. Travel evidently agreeing with him, he went farther afield to Rome, and on his return journey founded a Monastery which he left in the hands of the MacGill, most likely MacCille, sons of the sacred cell. There is no certainty of the location of the Monastery, but St. Ailbhe passed down Strathspey on his way back to Ireland. It is recorded that he left his boat in the North with the Dalriadans, among whom he had been of great use. Their King, Fintan Finn, had asked the Saint to help in retrieving his wife and children from the hands of the men of Connaught. St. Ailbhe did not take to arms for this purpose; he used instead present-day Tinkler methods of attack, and cursed the enemy so wholeheartedly that the Connaught men were weak of it and the family was restored.

In Ireland he settled his disciple St. Colman, whose name is in the Aberdeen Breviary, and then he went to visit St. Bridget of Kildare. Whether the religious colony founded by St. Ailbhe was the holy cell on the island of Alvie, a cell which later bore the name of St. Columba, cannot be proven ; but the Saint's disciple, St. Colman, had an adviser in St. Eatha whose two Chapels were in this same district.

St. Eatha was known as the St. Bridget of Munster ; and Bride or Bridget before she was Christianised was a goddess of fertility. That Eatha shared this value also may surely be concluded from the Gaelic feminine noun " Eite," " an unhusked ear of corn, or a replacement on a ploughshare." Just as St. Ailbhe, the son of Evil, can be traced back into early myth, so Eatha becomes kith of Keridwen, of Persephone and Isis. Of the other Chapels connected with Alvie, those of St. MacLuac at Balavil and Chapelpark leave no remaining trace, but the ruin of St. Drostan's Chapel at Dunachton is still preserved.

The present Church of Alvie has undergone many changes. It used to have a gallery and a sort of royal box on the side wall where the Duke and Duchess of Gordon sat above the tenantry, but on a level with the high pulpit opposite. Here, as perhaps in some other Speyside Churches, a Gaelic service used to be given, but it followed the English service which was attended by " the gentry." No such distinction should ever have been made. The Minister should have held on in the tongue of the people and of the native Lairds, and strangers could have learnt what it was to be blessed in the Gaelic and gone away the richer for the experience.

This Church opens its doors in the morning and

THE MONADH RUADH AND HUGH BARRIE'S CAIRN

(page 106)

closes them at night, keeping natural time with the surrounding water-lilies. The Tinklers wander in and out of the building, using the cupboards when the first frost makes it necessary to take the artificial flowers from the graves of their settled kindred, and visitors feel a welcome in the open porch that makes them conscious of an hospitable Deity; an understanding, loving Power who does not even scorn the little black kitten that finds a happy snoozing place in the dark recess of the wooden collection ladle.

Up to 1880 the Minister was not aware that there were more of his congregation below the pews than

CHURCH COLLECTION LADLE

in them, but when the floor was lifted for replacement, a hundred and fifty skeletons were discovered lying head to head. Out in the churchyard stands a cross on which is inscribed :

    " Who they were, when they lived, how they died,
        Tradition notes not.

    " Their bones are dust, their good swords rust,
        Their souls are with the Saints we trust."

While I join in the charitable faith regarding the destination of their souls, I deplore the superabundant trust that buried them without further investigation. What was the shape of the skulls? How old were the bones ? Why the suggestion of swords unless weapons were found ? If they were, where are they? Plague victims were often buried *en masse* in Churches, but they would not have swords and were as likely to be women as men.

Local tradition points to a battle having been fought in the vicinity, and is strengthened by the loch being reported as a haunt of the Bean Nighean, the phantom washer-wife. This eerie creature was seen by those doomed to die. She was counted to be the soul of some woman who had died at child-birth and whose clothes had not all been washed at the time of burial. Such a death was considered as unnatural and premature, and the soul had to wash the shirts of those about to be slain until the day came which would have been the date of her own natural passing.

When the Tumuli in the pine wood behind Dal-raddy Cottage were opened, human remains were found, with an accompaniment of sword-blades and buckles. The place is now no more than an in-exhaustible stone heap, which can easily spare the boulders from its warriors' graves for the neighbour-ing children to use for designs of gardens and plans of palaces. The outlines lie here and there, squares, triangles, and circles; patterned ground-plans which, should they miraculously rise in petrified beauty, would overtop the pine trees with magical towers.

When the railway was built, a skeleton was found with a pair of very large hart horns laid across it, and the Moor of Alvie disclosed Roman urns under small arches of half-burnt clay. If ghosts should rise in Alvie, what a fine ceilidh they could have! Pict and Roman, Hunter and Tinkler, presided over by the

Scandinavian King from Dunachton's height and the gay Duchess of Gordon. Was ever a monument so unrepresentative as that of the gay Duchess? Down by the river, remote even from the tree-lined carriage drive that winds to Kinrara, was indeed a strange spot for a lively person to choose, and the piece of masonry that acts as a monument is disappointing. It is not reasonable to expect a Taj Mahal, but the solid box, cornered with wide-based pyramids, has not even the suggestion of a door whereby the bright little spirit might escape to pirouette among the rabbits or play hide-and-seek with the deer among the solemn rhododendron bushes.

It seems strange that this lady who capered about the countryside in a phaeton drawn by gaily caparisoned goats should also have appreciated the peaceful loveliness of such a resting-place. What, I wonder, did this bonny recruiting sergeant know of St. Eatha that she should choose the Saint's Chapel site for her sleep? The Duchess's reward for the Gay Gordons was not a kiss; the shilling was taken from between her teeth. Even so, it must have been hard for many a glen lass to see her Ian " go foreign " on such coercion. A lovely and enchanting personality was admittedly the charm of the Lady Jane, but many a soldier's widow and many a sonless father must have disagreed with the famous description of the Duchess of Gordon as " the lady who combined everything which a man is able to imagine of excellence in a woman."

Alvie is said to have had a Castle on the mound of the promontory. Mention is made of it in con-

nection with a MacKintosh who murdered his Chief
at Dunachton, in the hope of taking his place.
Dunachton is but a short distance from the loch,
and yet the hopeful assassin sought safety no farther
away than the Castle. It was a misconceived notion
on his part, for he himself was slain and the Castle
burnt.

I felt sure that the great mound must have some
sign of such an edifice, and explored it thoroughly
in the unsought company of a red and white cow
whose snortings seemed to forebode some harassing
situation. My hopes and also my fears were
groundless. I could find no stone that was more
than a plain boulder, though the likelihood is that
the Manse and byre stand in the Castle's place and
old stones may have been used in their building ;
and I was assured that the cow was a friendly
creature only desiring company. In trying to find
the Castle and lose the cow I came across a spring
low down by the lapping water's edge. Unfor-
tunately it is neither very accessible nor reliable, so
that the water for the Manse is drawn under the loch
in pipes. The " cattle-spring " beside the road
that leads across the neck of land behaved as many
a Highland spring is said to have done. It ceased
to flow because it was offended. In other words,
when the road was under repair the weight of the
carts disturbed its functions and it has literally
moved elsewhere.

Above the loch, the hill known as the Broom or
the Swept-one, scoured as it is by the wholesome
besom of the Wind, shows a zig-zag track upon its
barren side. This is the peat track leading to the

Moss, where free peat could be had for the fetching. No wonder the carts no longer rumble and bang over the bare rocks and loose boulders that signified a road.   Even a tank might justifiably sulk at such a proposition.

At the foot of the gully where the boundary burn comes leaping to the loch, a hummock of turf-covered stones and a handful of nettles indicate the larach of a tailor's cottage.   This tailor added to his popularity in the houses where he worked by singing verses of his own composition in the Gaelic. That they were often " agin the landlord " did not detract from their charm for the tenantry, but it led to an order that he was to remove himself and his belongings clear of the estate.   He was an old man, and many, including the Minister, interceded on his behalf, but without avail.   So the tailor betook himself to the Laird of the adjoining estate, and explaining his difficulties, pointed out that verses of praise for a kindly landlord were just as easy to compose and more pleasure to sing.   The Laird smiled, and took on a new tenant, and the tailor rebuilt his home at a distance of about ten yards—just over the boundary burn—where he lived till his soul made the Last Flit across a wider water to be a permanent tenant of the Laird of Lairds.

The stone pillar that shoots from the Tor of Alvie, though it is useful as a director, being visible from Laggan to Grantown, is no addition to the beauty of the landscape.   If there is no originality in the monument itself with its inscriptions in the Gaelic, in English and Latin, in praise of the last Duke of Gordon, there was plenty of excitement

over its erection. The hauling of the material to
the height, and the continual combat against the
wind, was accepted by the workmen with fighting
spirit. When the copestone was reached they
" threw their caps into the air for joy." Nor were
they the only joyous ones, for it is reported that " the
monument was completed in a year to the joy of the
Building Committee." Moreover, this determination not to let grief get the upper hand remained
with the promoters, who, according to a newspaper
report of the time, ascended the hill on the day of
the ceremony armed with " plenty of mountain dew
which was drunk in solemn silence, after which the
procession returned in the same order to the place
whence it set out, and having there sat down, healths
were drunk with doffed bonnets." What time of
day this took place is not stated, but the company
met again at six in the evening " to dinner at the
Pitmain Inn where —— officiated as Croupier."
So stands the monument to the Cock o' the North,
and doubtless the local tale of treasure hid in the
Tor is an augmentation to the bottle of coins (1839)
which was enclosed in the foundations.

The Tor lies in the grounds of the Kinrara estate,
and there is another monument on its timbered side.
The Waterloo cairn commemorates the prowess of
the Gordon Highlanders at that battle, and it belongs
to the regiment, which is responsible for its upkeep.
As it is a war memorial the public are free to climb
the rocky path to its sheltered seat, but there is no
need for such distinction, as no hindrance is set to
wanderings on the estate. One is free to go past
the water-lily loch or round by the Bogach to the old

ford. At this crossing the carriage of the Duchess used to risk the flood to visit her friends at the Doune; and not so long ago, the carts returning from Perth with the Grant luggage when the family had been South rumbled and grated among the wonderful coloured pebbles, their drivers never quite at ease till the shingle of the east bank was reached, and the shadow of the ancient trees of Doune fell on the wooden and leather cases that had been their charge for three days.

The Highlands hold many a surprise. At an out-of-the-way croft, suggestive in every stone of a home untouched by modern thought, a piece of wire running from the chimney to the nearest larch may be responsible for a scornful attitude towards the legends of the district and its native tongue.

On the other hand, Alvie, in spite of its popular motor track, has preserved thoughts and tales precious and beautiful. There the Bodach Eighe-ach still sends his mournful death-note trembling through the night; stirring a prayer from bedded folk who rise to peep through slanting skylights at little green lights that wend their way through the darkness up the mound to the silent Cladh, where by that same token some soul is due to lie.

Here, one with "the Sight" saw a man carrying a coffin with a dog walking at his heel, and was therefore not surprised to hear of the death of a friend next day. The dead man possessed no dog of his own, so the animal must have been of the same litter as Anubis and the dog of Mexican myth who accompanied souls through the dark corridors on the other side of the grave.

In a little cottage near the farm of Dalraddy, Prince Charles is said to have rested on his way from Culloden, and the farm of Dalraddy itself is the place of the punctuation riddle :

" Bha cailleach ann Dail-radaidh
'S dh' ith i adag 's i marbh.

There was an old wife of Dalraddy who
Ate a haddock, being dead."

The farm is evidently fortunate in rations, for after the great flood had subsided, Mrs. Cumming discovered a pike, some trout, a hare, a turkey, potatoes and turnips all marooned on a little mound conveniently near the door !

Alvie and its merging partner Lynwilg are rich in stone circles, and the one at Delfour is still in wonderful condition, even though stones have been removed from its three great circles for additional material in the new houses on the estate.   At twelve o'clock on New Year's Eve these exiled stones make strange sounds described as " something of a growl with a scrape in it."   In late summer the wind rustles among the full oat-heads that sway like a green sea to the edge of the magic circle, accentuating the static silence of the grey stones that stare across the open fields, across the dark forest, to the jagged hills.   No need to look at a compass here to get bearings, for the tallest stone, broad at the base and tapering in height, always stands to the south.

I have heard it alluded to as " the Father," and reference to a faded belief that the standing stones were men who were petrified by some powerful curse joins up with the ancient tales of men who hid their souls in stones for safety, and with the suggestion that the souls entered the stones after death, making them represent the living family.

Circles and mounds stand at intervals all up the strath—from Raitts, to Kincraig, to Delfour, to Ballinluig beside Loch Alvie; there is one in the wood beside the house of Sir George Henschel the

STONE CIRCLE AT DELFOUR

famous singer, while Aviemore has one in a good state of preservation, and from it the circle at Loch nan Carraigean, which has the appearance of a foundation for a beehive building, is visible. The line then crosses to Pityoulish where incised stones lie by the wayside, taken from a circle in a field. There is another at Street of Kincardine with strange finger-length marks on it, and from there the view is open to Lynchurn where more incised stones were discovered. From the Tom-na-Croich remains of a circle to Inverallan is less than a mile and a half, and the latter place has stones incised with the same designs as are to be seen at Congash near Grantown. I have omitted the mounds at Avielochan as perhaps being of a different species, for a stone passage leads into one opened mound where a circle of binding stones acts as a wall to the little chamber, now open to the sky. Here were found a bracelet and a piece of jet, suggestive of travellers, since jet is not indigenous to Scotland. A second mound stands beside the opened one, with its secret intact.

Obviously some religion earlier than Christian, earlier than Culdee, earlier than Druid, flooded this strath; leaving monuments that appear to have been more lasting than its philosophy, though how much of the latter has been interwoven in each succeeding creed we cannot know.

Mr. Lewis Spence points out in his work on *The Mysteries of Britain* that "The stone circles of Britain were not built by the Druids, although the development of Druidism was associated with them." He alludes to their existence in the days of the new Stone and Iron Age when the Iberian race from North-West Africa brought the Cult of the Dead to Britain.

The arguments for and against the possible uses of the stones are as endless as the circles themselves. The fact that similar rings exist in India and that some of the incised designs on the Speyside stones coincide with creatures of the Byzantine Bestiaries or Picture-books, takes the question even farther afield than the connection between the scattered areas of Carnac and Caithness, of Orkney and Ireland.

To sit in the twilight beside the urgent dumbness

of the grey stones, watching the black and white flash of an oyster-catcher's flight and struggling to find some cue that shall conquer the silence of the ages, trying to ignore the irony of the bird's cry, " Bi glic, bi glic " (" Be wise, be wise ")—to do this continually is to court madness.   It is much safer to repeat the annoyed conclusion of the Rev. J. Longmuir that " We will say nothing more of these stones than that they have failed to hand down to us the event which they were erected to perpetuate." But can it, should it, rest at that?   Can we leave unravelled the secret of our earliest religious strivings while day by day the story is being erased by the elements or removed wholesale by those ignorant of its value?

The advance of the philosophy of a race is of equal, if not of greater, importance than its outer history of battle and kingship, and yet the protectors of Ancient Monuments, while carefully guarding castles which have yielded every word of their tale, leave the picture stones of Strathspey askew in the unshorn grass, a tempting prey for builders of byre and barn.

The Monadh Ruadh are hidden from Alvie by the Tor, but the road to Aviemore gives the grandest view in the strath, for it shows the spread of Glenmore like a great bay, undulating with trees and backed by barren peaks.   On the left the hump of the southern Craigellachie hides the stretch of country to Abernethy.   This Crag-of-the-Alarm is not very high, but it served its purpose as a beacon to fetch Grants from far and near ready-armed for any fray.

How many thousands of times the name must have been said, and with what varied sentiments. Whispered with distress and foreboding by the wife who caught sight of the flicker of flame from her cottage door; repeated by her in dismay to her Goodman, who would be instantly to his feet with a note of excitement in the cry " Craigellachie ! " Up and down the strath the word would ring till in the shadow of the hill all the manhood of the glen would be massed in expectancy, and far-off foes would be sharpening their swords to the sound of the name hissed in revenge or whispered with fear.

The sixteenth century would find the Grant gathering dressed in the simple big plaid, but in 1704 the Chief commanded that " tenants, cottars, maltmen, tradesmen and servants should provide themselves with Highland trews, coats, short hose of tartan, of red and green set, broad-sprigged, with sword, pistol and dirk." This was an inconvenient attire by comparison, especially for the Grants who had to ford the Spey from Rothiemurchus lying opposite the Crag.

ROUND ROTHIEMURCHUS

Loch an Eilein is the show-place of Rothiemurchus.
It is strange that praise and appreciation should be
capable of spoiling a place as it may spoil a person.
A loch cannot look superior and an island cannot
preen itself; and yet Loch an Eilein, lying behind
the birch-clad Ord Ban, reflecting the big hills of
the east, encircled with dark fir, dressed with
water-lilies and bejewelled with a castled island, is
spoilt by popularity. Or is it just some hidden
desire in myself to obliterate all traces of mankind?

Country people, a horse, even a horse and cart, do
not disturb the unity of Loch an Eilein, but anything
in the shape of a car, whether it be the grocer's van
or a Rolls Royce, is as incongruous as a bowler or
lum hat worn in conjunction with a kilt. Town
shoes, perched precariously among the roots of the
ancient trees that edge the water, fill me with a sense
of shame. I can find no logical reason why people
should not come in cars, and no excuse for my un-
sociable attitude, but at the sight of them I hastily
retire, like the osprey ever driven to farther retreats.
They are not rowdies who come to Loch an Eilein,
they do not leave peel and papers about, but they do
scatter the litter of their minds. " Awfully jollies "
and " dashed fines " and " stunnings " and " by
joves " lie about in the air, more conspicuously than
cigarette-ends on the turf. The time to see the loch

is in the spring, before the swallows and the visitors arrive.

To come up the deep-rutted road from opposite the Doune, or over the hill by Inverdruie, is to tip-toe into a private nursery. Everything is young. The weeping birches of Ord Ban swing a myriad emerald discs from their trailing twigs. Young lambs, young rabbits, fledgelings, and foals are all contentedly at play and take no exception to a little additional company. Winter still frowns down from the snow-capped heights, but the sun favours this sheltered spot, and spring can afford to be a bit coquettish, with a flash of cherry blossom here and a sprinkle of fallen stars disguised as wood-anemones among last year's dead leaves.

By October, too, the place has recovered its pristine loveliness. The air has been washed in the amber of autumn sunshine. Ord Ban has changed to a magic hill scintillating with the gold of faerie coinage ; the cottage gardens flame with the last red berries of the guelder rose, and even the little island has its treasury, for yellowing ash and willow have filled the Castle chambers with aureate beauty.

In winter what a difference ! Not a vestige of colour is to be seen. Only the dazzling white of the snow, the sudden dark among the sheltered stems of the forest, the long grey sheet of ice seeming to hold an island that could be pushed about over the shining surface, and from the centre of the Castle the naked arms of the ash, erect and defiant, like the gaunt figure of Grizzel Mhor. There is no tradition of her gauntness, but the name suggests it. Brave and resourceful she certainly was in her defence of the island against General Buchan, who had hoped to raze the building to water-level in the absence of the Laird. All honour to Grizzel, though her situation was not very desperate, for an island is an obstinate object of attack, as the Wolf of Badenoch knew when he repaired the Castle; as the Comyns before him knew; as others, right back to the original owners, were well aware. The Crannog-makers who enlarged the island by building out on piles also drove a secret zig-zag course-way a few feet below water from the island to the shore. The pattern of this road to the Castle only three living people were allowed to know at a time. For some reason they have failed to hand on the knowledge, and no one can find the way to the Castle now except by boat.

Some folk find a Yale lock a sufficiently complicated method of getting into their house late at night. Imagine having to essay a hidden zig-zag causeway by the light of the stars, and think of the perilous if deserved results of zigging when it was a zag, or zagging when it should have been a zig! The last occupants of the Castle-island were probably the only ones who were able to see the hidden course, and they had no need of it—the ospreys.

After having used the residence for years, they went South and never returned. "Heids of Departments" young Jim suggested, but it is thought that a pair shot in the New Forest may have been the Loch an Eilein birds on their southward migration. Now that Captain Knight has introduced the osprey into Scotland again, perhaps a new pair will build on the branch or two that remains of the old nest, even if it is only to oblige the 'bus driver who has persistently kept the description of Loch an Eilein displayed as " The Home of the Ospreys "; keeping the nest warm as it were, against the family's return.

No one may enter the little black door of the Castle where it opens straight off the water; but, standing on a certain stone, with face low to the loch, your voice will run like a water-beetle over the intervening space, and tumbling through the door, shout back at you with increased vigour. " Am bheil thu aig an tigh Alasdair Mac an Righ? " followed by groans, is very effective as a solo, but " 'Ello Woof, are yew at 'ome? " seems to leave the loch a little colder, and the ripples are like shudders as they lap the shore.

To the south-east across the waters Sgoran Dubh, Braeriach, and Cairngorm lie ranged, and a lovely walk winds in that direction, past the monument to General Rice who was drowned whilst skating, to Loch Gamhna. Known as the Stirk's Loch, probably because it lay near the Cattle-raider's Road, this stretch of water is noted in the summer season for its water-lilies. They lie, hundreds of them, white lamps among the dull surface leaves, creating a little legendary world of their own, so different from the surrounding hardness of the rocks and the tangle of the heather.

From here a path leads up to a hole that was at one time the retreat of a wild cat, and of something even more vicious—a man known as " Black Sandy." Whether his hair was black I do not know, but black was his deed in cutting off the ears of the

THE TINKLERS' CAMP

(page 112)

bonny housekeeper at the Croft. Like a lot of people who do queer things, Sandy thought he had a good and sufficient reason for mutilating the lady whose charms had already accounted for three or four children to the young Laird. The Croft that lies between Inverdruie and the Loch an Eilein was a fine property, and the old Laird at the Doune had no mind for it to be parcelled out to the housekeeper and her children, and gave Sandy leave to stop the wasting of the heritage as best he might.

It is not fair to judge those days by a modern standard, for they lay nearer to the times when a Chief was the Father of his people, when the eldest legitimate son was given to a foster-mother until the age of fifteen, and all such ties were used to bind the loyalty of the Clan, so necessary to the safety of one small community against another.

The villain of Cat's Den, however, felt it his duty to serve the old Laird as best he could, but he did not find Rothiemurchus a very healthy district after the deed, and disappeared towards Grantown. Having nearly murdered another man there, he returned to his old haunts, but being rather uncertain of his popularity, he used the Cat's Den as his home. From there he jumped farther afield, to America, where one of his descendants became a President of the United States.

The Croft is still inhabited, but the ruins of its bigger buildings stand windowless on the height of the sweet-pastured hill where the sound of the cowbells' mellow " Clong-clong " sounds all day in reply to the plover's keening. There is a fine old tree by the roadside, so old that perhaps it remembers

F

the first builder who made use of this clearing in the forest, and dreams of its companions that once stood thick-set about the house, though it can know no more than we do about the ring and cup marks in the neighbouring rock.

It would be at the time when there was no house but a fort at the Doune that the Shaws lost Rothiemurchus to the Comyns.   Foreseeing the worst for her Chief and his whole family, the nurse stole away with the little heir in her arms, just before the attack.   Right across the wild country, with fear of cateran and Comyn ever at her heels and a crying baby at her breast, the woman went till she came to the Castle of the Baron of Strathardle in Perthshire. The Baron, being friendly with the Shaws, listened to the tale with sympathy and offered to take the child and bring the boy up as his own son.   Satisfied with this success, the foster-mother returned to her own country.   Just as she expected, there was now no sign of Shaw at Rothiemurchus ; those who had not been killed had been obliged to flee, and the Comyns ruled the forest land undisturbed.

The foster-mother knew her danger, and chose to live alone behind a well-barred door.   Years went by as she lived through day after day at her simple duties ; tending her cow and sitting to the wheel at dusk, twisting with the pull and turn of the wool thoughts and hopes of the absent boy who carried the fortunes of Rothiemurchus.   Then came a night when the long sigh of the wind was contrasted by a sharp rapping at the door.   The cow was in, the bolts were fast ; but even so, it was a moment to call upon the mercy of the Holy Virgin when the

Comyns came to call. There was more than one
visitor outside by the sound of whispering. A voice
was raised. "It is I, your foster-son, the young
Shaw."

Joy and caution fought in the woman's agitated
mind.

" I would know the breath of that one," she called.
" Let him put his lips to the hole in the door."

"No, no," she moaned on trying the experiment,
"that is not the life-breath of the little one I held
as mine."

" That was a foul jest," remonstrated a voice.
" Try now, mother."

Once more the trembling woman bent her head
to the door, and then flung it wide with a cry of joy
to admit young Shaw and his bodyguard.

They were only a small company, though they
filled the little cottage to bursting-point, but they
were keen for revenge, and most of the Comyns
being away on a foraging expedition, the moment
seemed propitious for attack.

The old woman's cow served for a night of feast-
ing, and guided by her knowledge of the enemy's
whereabouts, the attack was successful and once
again the Shaws held the land.

Some say that the Comyns destroyed the fort of
Doune that stood on the top of the boat-shaped
mound beside the Spey at Rothiemurchus, and
others contend that Patrick Grant razed it when he
took the property. One thing is certain, that whoever reduced it left a curse upon the next builder
using the site, and that is why the present house
is situated not on but at the foot of the hillock.

Patrick Grant began his reign over Rothiemurchus from the house of Dell which he built at Inverdruie, and the tale of his coming is a tragic one.

The Doune was a happy place in the time of the widow Shaw and the young Laird Alan, her son, till the coming of Sir John Dallas. He came as the Widow's second husband, and thus ousted the young heir. It was a difficult situation even for a man who might have been willing to make allowances for the boy's jealousy, and Sir John was not disposed to do that. There were faults on both sides, and the mother was unable to heal the breach, so the youth spent most of his time hunting in the forest with his favourite dogs.

One evening, on the way back from the chase, one of Alan Shaw's dogs turned into the Smiddy and was at once sent flying out on the toe of the step-father's boot.

The cry of the hurt dog, the elder man's sneer, and the sting of the insult before the company gathered at the door, just served to light the flame of a smouldering murderous instinct, and in the place now known as Dalaisith, the place of Strife, Shaw killed his step-father. From that ground, year by year on the anniversary of the deed, a strange scent rises. The smell of autumn you might say, except for the strength of it, except for some maddening taint about it, something evasive and mercifully unusual—for it is the scent of blood !

To imagine Alan horrified at his own deed would be a mistake. He, a Shaw, the rightful Laird of Rothiemurchus, to give up his heritage and be treated with scorn? With a hack of the sword, off came the Dallas head to swing by the hair as Alan carried it dripping to the house of Doune and showed it to his mother. Few sons would have done as he did, and fewer mothers would have stood the shock as did the Lady Dallas, for she gave up the title-deeds to the Crown and insisted that her son be disinherited and outlawed. Alan only spent a few months in the forest before he died, leaving the firs of Rothiemurchus to hold yet another shadow, a lone figure, a plaid drawn over his face, a dog at his heel. If it is possible to cast comfort over the river of Death, across the span of years, then as I tramp the winding road or the deep woods of Rothiemurchus, Alan Shaw may sometimes feel an easing of the heart.

'Tis an ill wind indeed that blows nobody good, and in this case the tragedy left the Chief of Grant in a position to offer the lands of Rothiemurchus to his son Patrick of Muckrach, " gin he could hold them." Patrick was ready to try holding them, and built the house at Dell which he decorated with the lintel stone from his castle of Muckrach, on which was carved, " In god is al my traist, 1598."

It was a later Laird who built the house of Doune where it stands overlooking the wide meadow land, its face to the hills, its back to the river and the deserted mound.

If the family deserted the mound there was said to be one person who did not. This was a Brownie who issued forth at night to assist the servants in the house, and to tinker the pots and pans in return for a regular supply of milk. After folks were bedded he could be heard, " Clink, clink, clink," till one

night a disgruntled Laird shouted at the Brownie to
" stop the din and let folk sleep ! "   There was a
sudden silence, and never again was the Brownie
heard, never was the hearth found cleaned for the
morning, or the coggies scoured, or the leaking pot
mended in its place.   The mound has the appearance of a barrow, and probably the work of some
ancient bronze worker is perpetuated in the tale of
the metal-hammering Brownie.   There are matters
in the Kirkyard of Rothiemurchus that seem connected with the Doune hillock, and the best way to
find the Church is from the road that runs along the
higher woods on its way to Feshie Bridge.

If the Church of Insh is surprisingly high up, the
Church of Rothiemurchus is surprisingly low down.
A path across an open field leads to tree tops, and
then drops suddenly among them to the little open
Cladh where the white Church sits askew beside
the river.   A beech hedge surrounds the gateless
acre, and brown sheep, seeming to have borrowed
their tint from the russet leaves, give sudden life to
the still scene.

On a recumbent grave slab are set five stones,
similar in shape to a kebbuck of cheese, and woe
betide whoever shall remove them !   The grave is
that of Farquer Shaw who " led and was one of the
30 of this Clan who defeated the 30 Davidsons of
Inverhavon on the North Insh of Perth 1390.   He
died 1405."   It reads still as a challenge.   One to
one in fair fight, and the word " defeated " shouts
like a bellowing stag.   I am not related to the
Davidsons, but I cannot read that stone without my
breath coming faster and a great strength rising in

me. The round stones, I was told, had "always
been there." It is obvious that they cannot have
been on that particular slab prior to 1405. From
their shape, which coincides with the shape of those
upon the tomb of Diarmaid in Glen Shee, they were
probably burial-stones from the mound of Doune,
which would account also for their magic powers of
returning to the grave if taken away, and the result-
ing curse upon the meddler. There have been
those who were ready to take the risk, among them
the Duke of Bedford's footman. He threw one
stone into the river, and though he was made to
replace it almost at once, he was drowned fording the
Spey that same week, and is buried in the Churchyard. At a later date two other men moved the
stones, and both died within the year.

If the Judgment Day should prove as literally
dramatic as some folk would have us believe, the
Cladh of Rothiemurchus will yet be the scene of a
fine stramash, though one man definitely arranged
for his grave to be in a far corner that he might up
and flee before the Shaws should get him! During
the time when the Shaws were still trying to regain
their hold of Rothiemurchus, their Chief was killed
in a fight against the Grants. It put an end for a
little time to their hope of regaining the property,
but they presumed that the Graveyard at least did
not belong to the Grants only, and they buried their
Chief with all honours. The Laird of Grant
thought differently, and the morning after the
funeral, when the widow opened the door of her
house of Dalnavert, the corpse of her lately buried
husband fell into her arms! He was duly buried

again, and again he seemingly rose from the grave
to stand upon his own threshold. This continued
day after day, till at last the resentful Laird of Grant
was obliged to give in and allow burial. He insisted, however, that the new burial should not be
where the Shaws had chosen. The new place of
burial was inside the Church under the pew of
Grant, where the Laird could stamp his disdain on
to the face of his enemy every Sabbath day during
service.

The ground is full of Grants, but of special
interest are the graves of the two Patricks, Patrick
the First who came from Muckrach, and Patrick
MacAlpine, so called because of his friendly rela-
tionships with the MacGregors.

He was an outstanding figure even in those days
of individuality, " tall and strongly made, and very
handsome, and a beau ; his trews were laced down
the sides with gold, the brogues on his beautifully-
formed feet were lined and trimmed with feathers ;
his hands, as soft and as white as a lady's, and models
as to shape, could draw blood from the fingernails
of any other hand they grasped, and they were so
flexible they could be bent back to form a cup which
would hold a tablespoonful of water." [1]   He would
drink no other water than that of the Lady-well of
Tullochgrue, and his health would seem to have
justified his choice, for he lived to be ninety-two,
after having married twice. His first wife gave him
three sons, and when she died he set out, at the age
of seventy-eight, to seek another. Even in that he
behaved like a figure in a faerie tale, for, hearing that

[1] *Memoirs of a Highland Lady*, Elizabeth Grant of Rothiemurchus.

Grant of Tullochgorm had some fine daughters, he requested the hand of whichever one might take his fancy. On the entrance of the eldest girl, Mac-Alpine asked her, if she had a tocher of gold as big as Craigowrie what she would do with it. To purchase dresses and jewels seemed to her a reasonable expenditure. MacAlpine frowned. The second and the third daughter responded likewise, and it looked as though the journey had been a fruitless one.

" Have you not another daughter? " he enquired. Tullochgorm explained that he had, but that she was out with the cows. On being fetched, Rachel looked amazed at the question put to her. " That is too hard a question for me," she replied. "I would take the advice of my husband as to what to do." So Rachel wed the great MacAlpine and came to Rothiemurchus. For her he built the house of the Doune, much altered since, of course, and no doubt she was happy among her household, superintending the preparation of wool and weaving, the dairy and the linen chests, and tending her own four boys. When her husband died, matters were different. She who was ever ready to " take the advice of her husband " found herself and her children badly treated at the hands of her eldest step-son and his wife. One day at Church, having received some further slight as she sat alone in MacAlpine's pew, the little lady felt near the end of her tether. Going up to her husband's grave as the Kirk scaled, she took off her high-heeled shoe, and beating the stone with it cried, " MacAlpine, MacAlpine, Rise up for ae half hour and see me richted "; but MacAlpine lay still: he had earned his rest, though it had come ignominiously, for Death had first stolen his big toe, which mortified after a slight wound, and through it claimed the rest of the great brave body.

Rothiemurchus is a silent place. Even the village of Inverdruie, with its School and Smiddy, is quiet. In the spring a young pear tree, apearl with snowy blossom, is poised tiptoe, showering her petals in laughter at the solemn regard of the dark-hooded pine trees that ring the village green. From the glistening windows of Inverdruie House the ghost of Captain Grant looks down on the star-spread ways. He could take the road to Coylum or go over the timber bridge to the Dell, keeping an eye on the course of the river Druie, for as it changes so do the fortunes of the Grants of Rothiemurchus take a turn. He could take the hill road to the Croft or go down the shadowed avenue of ancient spruce that leads over the Spey to Aviemore, with a snort of scorn for modern tennis-courts and a raised eyebrow at the new Church that has taken so long to rise from its foundation, but with a smile of gladness at the familiar churr of the sawmill and a feeling of comfort at the coo of cushats in the trees.

AMONG STRANGE FOLK

THE SONG OF THE DAOINE SITH

We sing in trailing sounds
Tunes made at the beginning
Of the pleating of the Winds
On the bare mountain sides;
We gather little herds
Of the sheep clouds, and the ringing
Of their silver bells is echoed
Where the yellow adder hides.

With hands of snowy feathers
And our green hair stringing,
In and out the loch we go
Upon the silver tides,
As we sing in trailing sounds
Tunes made at the beginning
Of the pleating of the Winds
On the bare mountain sides.

The road from Inverdruie to Loch Morlich runs among pine trees to Coylum Bridge, and there in the summer the little Post Office garden is almost a shock, so replete is it with every possible flower; an oasis of domestic cultivation in the surrounding undisciplined moor and wood. Purple Monk's-hood and Pansy, Poppy and Candytuft riot together, and the Marigold, flower of Beltane, blazes its miniature suns among the Nasturtiums and Sweet William. Roses red and roses white climb over the house, more like a shower from heaven than a growth from earth, and the bees' murmuring hymn of delight can be heard as you lean over the stone bridge to watch the broil of the river.

The stream is born in Loch Eanaich, and beside its source was also born a son to the Laird of Grant. He it was who spanned the river with this bridge at the place known before as Cuing Leam, the narrow leap, now spelt Coylum.

I wonder if the Bodach Cleocain Deirg of Coylum, the man of the little red cloak, helped travellers over the chasm, or whether being of the goblin tribe he gathered treasure from the unfortunates who fell in. The Bodach of Coylum is almost forgotten now, all information about him begins with " I remember hearing of him ever and ever so long ago." So the scarlet of his little cloak is fading till even those with the most retentive memories will soon not be able to catch the tint of his strange raiment among the shadows of rock and bridge.

Soon after crossing the bridge, the road leads across an open moor where dead trees stand in alarming nakedness, the smooth whiteness of their unbarked limbs defying distance and throwing them unnaturally near from the dark background of mountain and heather. I have seen the hills from here so deep in tone that they matched a rich navy blue, and on a different occasion so ethereal that they seemed only sky-dreams. The path mounts to an ever-widening view where the unchallenged wind hurls itself over the heather and retreats roaring into the forest that soon devours the track. Just before the shelter of the woodland a bypath leads to a renowned well. It would be easy enough to find,

even were there no path at all, for not only is the
vegetation discoloured to a yellow tinge for yards
around, but also the atmosphere is permeated with
an odour that may be designated by all the offensive
names pertaining to the word " smell "; unless, of
course, one happens to like the scent of sulphur.

In past days, ailing people from Braemar tramped
the twenty-eight miles through the Lairig to drink
its healing waters, wished themselves well, and left
a silver coin by way of an offering.   Doubtless
kings and nobles took their dose at the spring too,
for Glenmore was a Royal forest at one time and was
later the hunting-ground of the Barons of Kincardine.   The latter would know where they could
get a sweeter drink, half a mile up stream, to take
the taste away.

Seen from the shadow of the surrounding wood,
Loch Morlich in the sun is as a great silver sword ;
the mile of its blade screened from the solemn
contemplation of the hills by countless dark-plumed
trees.   The mountains seem to move suddenly
nearer as one emerges from the forest to the full
view of their downward sweep and primal upheav-
ings, their crusty indentations intensified by the
unrippled surface of the loch.   Creag an Leth-coin,
Sron na Lairige, Braeriach, Carn Lochan, Carn Toul,
and Ben MacDhui, they stand like a gathering of
warrior-heroes, kithless relics of a forgotten saga.

The foot-hills are bare now where once great trees
grew, for in 1736 the forest was cut and cleared by
a merchant of Hull to whom the Duke of Gordon
sold the timber.   The wood was floated down the
Spey on rafts and there converted into " forty-seven

sail of ships of upwards 19,000 tons." The biggest vessel was fittingly called the "Glenmore." So the forest sailed away overseas as the property of the East India Company.

After this devastation, which took twenty-two years to complete, the forest grew again, covering the slopes with its bosky beauty, and again, in 1915, came the sound of the woodman's axe as the Canadian Forest Corps felled the timber for war purposes. The Forestry Commission has now purchased the land right up to the summit of Cairngorm, but there is a rival landowner who was there long before Governments or Lairds thought of exploiting timber. Domhnall Mor, King of the Faeries, has precedence at the western end of the loch, where his faerie dwellings, like glacier mounds, like giant graves, like miniature hills with the green of their magic undimmed, lie clear for all to see.

" The Shorter Catechism and Faerie stories were mixed up together to form the innermost faith of the Highlander," wrote Miss Grant of Rothiemurchus. It is a very reasonable mixture surely. For the Daoine Sith are the spirits of the dead, disembodied souls awaiting rebirth. The Faerie faith, surviving as it does in the Celtic lands of Scotland, Ireland, the Isle of Man, Cornwall, Brittany, and Slovakia, is in line with all other faiths in which angels and spirits hold their place, and only those who are ignorant of even the little that is known about psychic energy, and those who are blind to the beauty of the Celtic Tradition, will lift the nostril or raise the eyebrow in scorn. The Faeries of Glenmore are only a further illustration of the belief in that " something indestructible " of which sage and savage have been equally aware.

The two following instances of belief were given me by present-day people, the first concerned being a friend of the speaker and a man of whom every one spoke as being "reasonable and temperate."

Here beside Loch Morlich he heard the ghostly pipes in the distance. Being a man not easily turned out of his way, he proceeded nevertheless. As he drew nearer the music he strained to see the player; louder and louder yet came the roar of drones and the sweet piercing notes of the chanter, and still there was no sign of the piper. Louder yet, till the man was forced instinctively to step aside, though not a sign of life could he see, but as the pipes passed him the wind of the drones beat against his cheek !

"There is nothing in ' The Book,' " I was reminded, " that speaks against the Daoine Sith, and there are things which we know but do not fully comprehend," said one. " For why should my friends that are gone come to me in my sleep and forewarn me of storms and of other deaths ? There is a thing cannot be explained and yet it is true."

" My Father and my Mother," said one, " told me how they saw a great figure of a Laird standing in the forest with the bark of the trees showing through the belt of him. Would you not believe what your Mother and Father told you ? "

There is also the tale of Robin Og who heard the Faeries playing their pipes beside the sithean of Domhnall Mor. There is a way by which you may obtain faerie gifts, and Robin, knowing it, cried,

" Is leatsa so, is leamsa sin " (this is yours and that is mine), and threw his bonnet to the sound of their going. There and then they dropped their pipes, which in this particular case were very small, for the spirits can change both shape and size at will.

Thrilled with his prize, the lad went home. How could he have hoped that a knitted bonnet would be a fair exchange for so precious an instrument? When he took the gift from the shelter of his coat, he found lying in his trembling hand only a broken blade of grass and a puff-ball.

It is easy to be scathing and incredulous about such matters within the sound of a dinner-gong, with the feel of solid furniture at one's back and the ring of voices talking about municipal elections, but to be alone in the long silence and the fading light by the sithean of Loch Morlich is another tale, and it is not easy there to still a louping heart when the heron calls or some small creature stirs among the heather.

If I had been asked which end of the loch to expect faeries I certainly would not have indicated the correct end, where the disused sluices hang upon rusty chains. I would have tramped the track that runs for over a mile beside the lapping water to the eastern end, which is fringed by a shore of snow-white sand. From there the view opens to the width and the length of the loch, with the mountains decreasing towards the west till they cease altogether, leaving the sheet of water divided from the sky only by a tiny border of trees; trees so diminished in the distance as to be unmeasurable even against a pinkie-

TOWARDS REBHOAN

(page 120)

nail, and beyond their tips no further rampart rises;
it is as if no more than a few blades of grass were
entrusted with embanking a deluge.

On the shore at hand an isolated tree, looking like
the grandfather of all the forest, stands crowning a
sand knoll; its unprotected roots gripping the

THE KEEPER'S CHILDREN

ground with twisted strands some twenty inches
round, then spraying into a million grotesque fingers
that cross and wind, split and dig, in the endeavour
to get a satisfactory hold. The wind has blown the
sand away, now on this side now on that, revealing
the intricate network but never succeeding in throwing the old tree half an inch off the straight. It
stands undaunted in perfect position where its dark

G

foliage cuts the light of the sky ; where the red of its
rugged bark enhances the silver blue of the water,
where its roots empattern the smooth white sand.
It is right for height, size, shape, and composition,
and is evidently the only thing that is unafraid to
share the night on the shore with the Bodach Lamh
Derg, the phantom with the red hand.   The Red
Hand !   It sounds both dreadful and romantic,
holding the thought of the Heroes of Ulster, of the
MacDonalds of the Isles, and even . . . of Mr.
Baldwin in Constantinople !   In the rôle of Reporter
many years ago, Mr. Baldwin asked permission of
the Turks to enter the sacred Mosque where no
Christian was allowed to set foot.   Having no
official card to help him, he offered the only im-
portant-looking piece of paper he had with him,
which happened to be an invitation to some Ulster
event with the Red Hand crested in the corner.
He was immediately granted admission, but went in
and came out without having noticed the reason of
this partiality, for the sign of the Red Hand is high
on a pillar where it was imprinted by Mahomet II.
as he stood upon the bodies of those slain in the
defence of the Mosque.   The mark is made in the
blood of those who so sacrificed themselves, and
over in Mexico a thousand similar ruddy signs
decorate walls and rocks.   There also the red was
the blood (or pigment to resemble it) of slaves
sacrificed to a deity.[1]

In Algeria it survives as a safeguard against the
evil eye, implying that the gods have been appeased.
Perhaps its widespread use shows it to be a natural

[1] *The Gods of Mexico*, Lewis Spence.

system of counting the dead, in the same way as the denounced but persistent method of using the fingers to assist addition has been, and still is, common to all countries.

The MacDonald hand that was flung ashore from a boat to gain possession of one of the Isles is more the tale of a severed hand than of a hand stained with blood, and seems too much of a local incident to connect with the Lamh Derg of Glenmore. The fact that the latter has sometimes been connected with the Barons of Kincardine is probably a confusion with the first Baron, who earned the title of the Red Knight; but the Lamh Derg who has for so long kept the domestic helpers of the Lodge on the right side of the door after sundown has only his right hand red with the gore of strangers whom he has killed for trespassing.

Hard as he was on strangers, he protected the deer, and Dr. Forsyth tells of an incident which shows him in this light.

Robin Og, son of one of the Barons of Kincardine, was hunting in Glenmore, and having killed a hind, proceeded to gralloch it. Happening to lay down his sgian dubh beside him, it disappeared. Then he took the knife from his dirk, and when he laid it down, it too vanished. Some time after, he met an old man on the sands of Loch Morlich wrapped in a grey plaid, but with one hand bloody and exposed. It was the Lamh Derg. " Is this you, Robin? " he said. " You are too often in the glen slaughtering my poor innocents. Do you remember the hind you killed in Glacan-bealaidh? You call it Glacan-bealaidh, but we call it Glacan-beadaidh. Here are your knives, but I counsel you to be more sober in the glen in future."[1]

The difference of meaning in the name is evidently the kernel of the remark, and " bealaidh " stands for a broom plant, while " beadaidh " signifies " impertinence."

To gather all the evidence is to find that the work of the Lamh Derg was to supply human sacrifice and to protect the deer, which is suggestive of service to a sylvan god or goddess. The path the Spectre roved was through forest land, though by the time of Robin Og the timber must have been thinned if broom was growing in the favourite hunting corrie ; but the Lamh Derg's rebuke anent the impertinence of strangers suggests that it was sacred to his deity. The additional and important fact that this was the forest of " The Maiden Tree," and therefore of tree-worship, seems to me to weld the argument and displace the relationship to the Barons of Kincardine ; while a reference to the figure being attired in a soldier's red coat appears as an ornamentation of a much later date.

The personified deities of the Celts were many, and human sacrifice was an important part of ritual, especially to those gods identified with growth. It may be that the Lamh Derg is ready with Mahomet II., with Mexican and Arab, to mark the record of his offerings with the sign of the Red Hand.

The road past the Lodge mounts above the bog to the Pass of Rebhoan, and on the way one may turn aside to find a strange little cemetery where

[1] In the Shadow of Cairngorm, Dr. Forsyth.

cairns mark the graves of horses, and tombstones of about the right height for inquisitive rabbits to decipher, show the resting-places of favourite dogs. Each of the tiny stones bears a name, a date, and an epitaph.   Of one dog is said :

> " Gave that strength of feeling
>   Great above all human estimate ;
> Such is the use and noble end of friendship,
> To bear a part in every storm of fate
> And by dividing, make the lighter weight."

Each dog is coffined, and some, having died away from the glen, have travelled far to be laid among their comrades in the hills, where they may now chase the game unrestrained, and dash madly in wild circles over the short thyme-laced turf when the mood of " Let-me-be-daft " is insistent.

Below, half hidden by trees, the waters of Alt na Feithe sob and gurgle among the stones, and across the dip the Corrie of the Coffin lies in shadow with the crescent snow of Ciste Mearad slung on the summit of the Blue Mountain above. In summer as well as in winter the Cairngorm is beautified by this snowdrift, though it sometimes gets small enough to make one enquire about the affairs of the Grants, as their good fortune is dependent on the continued existence of this white patch.

It is nearly eight miles from Glenmore Lodge back to the comparative civilisation of Aviemore, and perhaps an extra two miles by the Raiders' Road, which strikes across the waste at the western end of the loch and bears away southward as if it intended to breast Carn Eilric, but dips where the forest is deep with underbrush of juniper.

The juniper is a strange growth.   No wonder it wended its way into faerie tales.   It cares not what the amount of space or the lack of it, but grows squat along the ground like a creeping thing, or tall and slender as a poplar, according to the advantages it finds.   Sometimes it is feathery and soft-foliaged with a strange bloom upon it, and sometimes it resembles whin in its punitive hardness of branch and thorn.   Who would think it worth while to garner the tiny blue berries to make gin, or the prickly tips for a shampoo rinse, though both are good concoctions?   But in the olden days its branches were burnt in every byre on New Year's Eve to keep the evil spirit of disease from the cattle —which it probably did, as it has slight disinfecting qualities.   It is still largely used in Norway for cleansing wooden casks.

In the Rothiemurchus forest the juniper mingles with heather, with ant-hills, with cranberry and blaeberry, leaving no choice of way but the Raiders' track, which runs from the direction of Lochaber whence the caterans came, and up to the Braes of Abernethy, where it is soon lost on its way to the coast.

Occasionally on the gradual descent the path dips beside open glades where the bracken has been tramped by the deer.   These little dells are such perfect resting-places, with patches of emerald grazing and perhaps a clear stream to slake the thirst, that one can understand the pleasure of the cateran's game, driving the ever-increasing herd from one such spot to the next. Thrilling work indeed, behind beasts who did not know the meaning of haste, who were liable to " low " for lost pastures and bring an angered mob to stop the passes. It was a long business this drive, not like the sudden foraging expedition before a marriage, when the feast depended on the booty, and the gay bridegroom headed the band. This was a larger and more serious undertaking, and the run from Lochaber was danger all the way, for the mountain barriers gave little choice of direction and only superiority of arms could bring success.

In consequence of the ceaseless raiding, the strath herdsmen were people of importance, and were known as Bowmen long after the weapon became an unnecessary part of their equipment. The loss of cattle meant loss of food, and to isolated crofting families it often meant death by starvation during the winter months. One of Robert the Second's grandsons became an adept cattle-lifter in this district ; indeed the band he headed was not particular to confine its attentions to herds, if better plunder offered a sporting chance.

Over these same rocks that break the path, down these hollows and over these dark ridges the caterans stepped, and not only their tracks remain but something more ; for here and there up and down the strath, between Kingussie and Grantown, one may meet men with merry devilment in their eyes. Men who speak with a refined enjoyment on the art of poaching, who can size up the points and value of a cow in the taking of a breath, and who expectorate inconspicuously when the Law is mentioned.

Caterans these, only kept in bounds by hobnail boots and cautious wives, and lack of congenial companionship.

Rathad nam Mearlach — the Thieves' Road — joins the path from the Lairig, and a further descent brings one to the confluence of the Druie and the Beanaidh, the combined waters mingling their joy in a sudden curving rush to a great open pasture.

The unexpected wealth of sky is like a gift after the close company of the trees. The wide, smooth ground is purple-breathed with gentian in July, their coloured spikes, so reluctant in their opening, dance right to the door of the long walled cottage that holds its skeleton timbers drearily to the sky. This unwindowed little house continues to give hospitality, though years have sighed past its doorless threshold since the family left it to follow their fate elsewhere; its walls still give shelter from the wind, and its fireplace boils many a kettle and tin for wanderers through the Lairig Pass.

On the high plateau across the stream stand the ruins of an older colony that was connected both with Rob Roy and the Laird of Rothiemurchus. The latter had a quarrel with the MacKintoshes concerning a mill, which ended in a threat from the Clan Chattan that the name of Grant should be utterly wiped out of the district. In desperation, for the enemy outnumbered his followers, the Laird of Grant asked the help of the MacGregors, and the appearance of Rob Roy and his men was sufficient to create a sudden scarcity of MacKintoshes.

In case his friend the Grant should be again molested, Rob Roy left two men to act as runners,

to bring him word to Balquhidder if further help
should be needed. Apparently these remaining
heroes made an enjoyable stay among the people
who were dependent on their fleetness, and one of
them married the Laird's natural daughter, Mairi
Bhuide, Golden-haired Mairi, who was not only

RUINED COTTAGE AT ALTDRU

beautiful but loved by old and young alike. The
Laird disapproved at first, but later showed his
forgiveness by giving them this croft of Altdru, and
here Mairi was often seen walking on the edge of
the forest with the hinds at her side, for she seemed
to have some magic power over them, so that they
would follow her, craving her caresses. The
descendants of the MacGregor runner farmed this
piece of land till 1890, and now the scene is one of

tumbled stones, of the mockery of nettles and wasted
pasture, where the hinds come down to feed and
find no Mairi to fondle their ears and call them
names that only hold their love and magic in the
Gaelic.

A new bridge, erected by the Cairngorm Club,
crosses the stream a little lower down, and the path
divides, one to run to Coylum and the other to Loch
an Eilein.   On a wooden signpost the ghost of a
message can just be traced :

> " To Kinrara and Lynwilg.
> *N.B.*—No boat on ferry at present."

To which information one may add, " not for the
last twenty years or so ! "   The heather-edged path
runs down to Coylum, and on to Inverdruie and
Aviemore, but a glance back before rounding the
hill where Barrie's cairn shines in the sunlight shows
such a panorama that the idea of Eternity seems
almost comprehensible.   With a tree here and a
tree there the forest begins, thickening to millions
and millions beyond count.   Heavy trunks and
twisted branches become lost in the brush of needle-
foliage, individual tree tops melting to a green sea
that streams up the sides of the hills, withdraws from
the steep Eilric to spread again over the broad braes
of Abernethy as an Atlantic tide washes a tiny bay.

THE ROADSIDE FIRE

THE Scottish Tinkler or Caird is not a Gypsy, nor a tramp, neither is he a tinker. In the use of the term Caird or Ceard, which is the Gaelic for " an artificer," is the token that the tousy-headed folk that you may see gathered by a fire at the wood of Dalraddy, or jogging along on a ramshackle cart, with precious little of either roof or raiment between them and the inclement weather, are the descendants of the metal-workers of older times. One has only to bear in mind the exquisite workmanship of the ancient brooches, as ornamental in the unseen parts as at the point of display, and the designs on old dirk handles and bracelets, to realise that the possession of such antecedents is no small honour; and though the Tinklers have descended from precious metals to tin and are now not even tin-workers, they still retain untarnished the honesty and courtesy of the cultured craftsman.

Their ranks were probably added to from time to time by Irish and by the men of the broken Clans, the outlaws and survivors of battles even before the disaster of Culloden. Both their names and their manners are far removed from anything characteristic of the Romany folk, who did not come over till about the sixteenth century, and though obviously there have been cases of intermarriage, those who know the difference in the ceremonies of the two tribes will deny its frequency.   As further proof of his descent from the Celtic artificers, some of the Tinklers are possessed of the words of a secret language called Shelta which has been traced back to connect with the ancient secret system of writing known as Ogham.   The language seems to be dying out, or is at least becoming mixed with "posh" and "deep" Romany and English tinker-slang.   Another sign of their antiquity lies in the use of a certain oath.   In extreme ire the Tinkler will explode with "By the Great Salmon ! "   This in no wise refers to poaching operations, for the Great Salmon leaps from early Celtic civilisation, when the belief was held that knowledge and poetry resided in a Salmon which inhabited a pool overshadowed by magic hazels whose boughs dropped nuts of Wisdom for the fish's sustenance.   A portrait of the Salmon may be seen on the Irish florin.   The Tinkler is well aware of the potency of the oath, and will not allow the use of it by his womenfolk.   Its meaning has not abated with age, and though he does not know its origin, the Tinkler keeps it for " occasions " when it is necessary to use something really emphatic, beside which modern blasphemies look pale.

The belief in the potency of curses, and the manner in which a Tinkler can give himself, and even more herself, up to malediction, is not necessarily a sign of low ancestry, unless it has deteriorated into vulgar abuse.   It was a weapon deliberately used in Druidic times by the Priests themselves, and the old books of Wales tell of immediate deaths as the direct result of poetic denunciation by persons of high lineage and estate.

" A Tinkler's Curse " is an item that has been underrated, at least from a point of view of rhetoric, for it was an ordinary Tinkler-wife on the Carr Bridge–Duthil road who shouted, " May the whole forest fall on you, may every stone jump up and hit your foot, may all your children die on you, and evil, evil, evil on you, and poison in your tinny ! "   The victim replied suitably, but with such a spate of words that I could not catch even the meaning of them.

The wanderers on Speyside might almost be divided as " the black " and " the red " haired, and three surnames would serve the lot.   To blame every dark-haired Tinkler with Gypsy blood would be ridiculous, there are plenty of other illustrations of the ancient Iberian stock to refute the charge; and the statement that the Scottish Tinkler women have a love of jewellery pointing to Gypsy origin is without foundation in the North, where it is quite exceptional to see them wearing anything other than plain gilt ear-rings, and those are donned more with the belief in their good effect upon eyesight than for purposes of adornment.

Whereas for centuries in the South of Scotland the Gypsies were most unjustly persecuted, the tinsmiths of the North fared better, for the Lairds not only made regular use of their services, but sometimes, as at Inverdruie, gave them a piece of land for their own.   On that triangular patch, now long in use as a gift from the Laird of Grant, is a cairn marking the grave of a wanderer who died when encamped there; and beside it a cleverly contrived home, a compromise between a Canadian shack and a round-topped army hut, has been occupied for more than two years by its builders, who reside there during the winter so that their children may attend the school.

Two hundred attendances per annum is the minimum allowed by law, and if the parents of a child over five years of age have not complied with these regulations, they can be denied guardianship and the child removed to an Industrial School. The Tinklers look upon " the Industrial " as a brick hell superintended by stern matrons with reasonless rules against freedom, people who cannot understand that if a lintie could get out of a cage by telling lies it would not long be the wrong side of the wire door. When I see the orderly ranks of some such school I remember the words of a Tinkler whom I met encamped with his small son on a windy moor, a most unsheltered situation, even for such folk. His indignant description of the institution which could lawfully have claimed his boy ran, " A place where they teach them to get dirty every day—real dirt, mind you—dirt on their hands and in their noses till they cannot breathe. Where they get it from Heaven only knows ! " Admitting the difference in cleanliness of atmosphere between town and country, but without going so far in condemnation, surely it is too much to expect that a nomad's child should at once adapt itself to the use of captured water, filtered sunshine, and regulated air, along with physical and mental restrictions that must be nothing short of torment. Perhaps some day the Education Authority will approach the matter in another way, by supplying winter caravans which can gather into settlements where simple education and craft work can be taught. The greatest difficulty would be to find teachers whom the Tinklers would like. Few people respect the background and observe the politeness which these folk expect. I have seen a man and woman get out of a luxurious car and go straight up to the camp fire, and follow this first offence by sitting down unbidden facing the opening of a tent, thus ignoring three rules which should be unconsciously kept by natural courtesy.

It is not perhaps quite so obvious that one should not ask the name of the host or hostess; but if on such an occasion the conversation is abruptly turned into another channel, it is not right to draw conclusions regarding dishonesty. It would be just as reasonable to argue that the great god Ra must have been a thief because he did his best to keep the knowledge of his name from Isis. Jehovah is not a name; and to this day the people of many tribes and nations do not make use of a child's name until it has reached a certain age, lest the use of it should transfer power over the child's soul to the speaker. Is there not a sense of dignity in the reluctance to tell the family history to the first comer?

"'Whence didst thou come?'

'I am from behind me.'

'Whither art thou going?'

'I am going before me.'

That is the answer of the Castle man."

Some of the Cairds are fairly wealthy, but many are reduced to a desperate state of poverty through the mass production of tinware; ware so cheap that there is not enough tin in it even to make it worth a Tinkler's while to melt down old pots and pans. Many have therefore become hawkers, but the difference in status between a creator and a vendor remains ; and a maker of heather pot-cleaners is above the seller of more pretentious goods.

Even hawking unreliable articles does not necessarily spoil honesty. A woman came to the door of a farm with a basketful of very cheaply manufactured billy-tins. When her persistent cajolery had resulted in a question regarding price, she remarked cheerfully, " Cheap at the money, lady, cheap at the money," but added in sudden conscientious confidence, " but mind you, lady, I put no faith in them myself."

Who would grudge her an apronful of potatoes or a pickle o' meal after that ?

The Tinklers get the name of being lazy because they do not strive to alter their circumstances. They are lazy ; but it is difficult for them to make a good living without going against their roving instincts. One may not quite understand the intense desire to " move on," but one has to admit the force of it when an old woman, knowing that she has but a few days to live, will insist on breaking camp to get over the next hill for no perceptible reason. I have never heard them praise the wonderful scenery in which they live, but can appreciation go farther than preferring the rigours of winter in a cave or under faulty canvas rather than enjoy the comforts of a house?

On Speyside the camps under the pines or in the shelter of quarries seem untidy and poverty-stricken

OLD CARR BRIDGE

(page 142)

affairs. The children, clad in a bit of everything, crawl out of the sleeping-hoods which are made from curved withies covered also with a bit of everything and anything, and a passing glance gives a decidedly bad impression.

If you look closer you will find that the " bits of everything " have been washed and thrashed by water and wind to a state as fresh as the herbage itself. That the uncut heads of hair are combed and clean, that the bedding is of fresh grass, that the horse is kept away from the camp and is regularly groomed. What would people in such poverty be like in the slums? What *are* they like, when occasionally a very severe winter combined with ill-health drives them to town lodging-houses? There was one such lived for some years in Perth ; and between public-houses and publicity, he forgot the code of the open road and descended the last steps of the social stair as a clown falls down a ladder.

" Keep away from me, Tinkler Jock," said a man, brushing his own coat sleeve that had come in contact with the beggar. Whether or not the implied insult was justified, old Jock pretended to rapidly search his muffler, and with a suggestive outflinging of the hand cried, " There 's ane wi' pink een for you ! " Such is the effect of town life on people who, if left in their natural surroundings, are clean and healthy and moral.

One wandering clan on Speyside is descended from the Tinkler Stewart of Atholl, who, in the disturbed days, saw a MacDonald in straits because his followers were dismayed at the onslaught of

some Covenanters.   Joining in the fray on behalf
of the MacDonald, this son of the tribe of Clout the
Cauldron laid about him with such effect that the
enemy was put to rout.

"Who are you?" asked the amazed and grateful
MacDonald.

"I am but a Ceard," was the reply.   MacDonald
knew better than to press the question, but turning
to his followers he said, "'Tis a pity you were not
all Tinklers this day."

From Somewhere in France, in the month of
October 1917, under circumstances hardly war-
ranted to make one appreciative of the blessings of
open-air life, Mr. Andrew M'Cormick wrote his
opinion of Tinklers for the Government Report on
Tinkers in Scotland.

"They are not the only people," says Mr.
M'Cormick in their defence, "who do not conform
absolutely to the law, and many such have got it
altered to suit the benefit of themselves and the
community."

Against the suggestion of bringing the nomads
into touch with town life, he says, "It would be
much more beneficial to insist upon slum dwellers
vacating their dens of iniquity in the fine weather to
come out and live in the open."   "You can hardly
expect," he adds of the Tinklers, "that they should
give up their loved freedom and their calling in order
to get the educational advantages offered.   You
might as well promise an eagle that if it would come
and be caged you would cut its tongue with a silver
sixpence and teach it to talk."

I quote a man of education, thought, and experience, because I am well aware that in trying to erase the mistaken idea of the Scottish Tinkler I lay myself open to the suspicion of roving blood in my veins, if nothing worse, by those who are unacquainted with the background and the actual facts of the wanderers' lives; just as the linguist cherishing the Scots tongue is suspected by the well-to-do grocer with no ear for its beauties.

On the North Road by the Spey one meets the Tinks in summer time, a routh of children perched high on a cart of grass that has been cut by the wayside for the horse. The father leads the animal, and the mother calls at the doors with a request for a spoonful of tea for the " blackie," or to sell some ware or buy a rabbit skin.

I remember near Croftgowan seeing some Tinklers who had taken to a car instead of a cart. The machine looked as if it had been salved from the loch after long immersion, and was, not surprisingly, stuck at the foot of the brae. The elder man pushed aside the skins that decorated the lamp in order to descend into the rain to " wind her a wee," while the young driver anxiously applied his small experience of mechanics to the gadgets beneath his hand. The hood of the car bulged downwards, its load of tinware and rags tied overhead with a network of rope and string, and in the dicky at the back Grannie crouched beneath her shawl with a child on her lap, her face a study of suppressed fear. The bonnet was lifted, and the rain from the old man's hat hissed upon the hot engine. If the car had gleeful memories of the panic of former owners on such occasions, if it expected a chorus of anxious voices—" Can't you *do* something ? "   " But we *must* get there "—it was grievously mistaken, for the Tinklers wasted neither breath nor trouble. They cheerfully backed it to the bottom of the brae, and in the shelter of a quarry settled themselves comfortably for the night.   They were only roving, and six miles this way, six miles that, it was all the same to them.

The Inverness-shire Tinklers do not go into Aberdeen or down to Perth ; their direction generally lies more towards Sutherland and Ross, keeping to the main routes until the signs of coming snow drive them back to their own winter haunts.   The traffic-haunted roads naturally offer the best livelihood, but that does not keep the traders from the by-ways if the mood and the money agree, as is shown by a tale of a Tinkler-camp in the wilds of Abernethy.   The Pass of Rebhoan is indeed a retreat from the world.

From Forest Lodge of Abernethy, on a day in early autumn, I followed the forest path towards Rynettan, delayed every few steps by the tempting blaeberries in their coats of bloom.   One generally has to keep a look-out for blaeberries, but on Speyside they are so big that they seem to look at you, and like the plenteous raspberry on the lower ground, the eating of them has nothing to do with appetite.   As I dropped from the bare height of the croft of Rynettan to the shadow of the burn, I gave a backward glance at the larach of Inchtomach, for there must have been something strange there once —something queer there must have been about this place down by the Nethy water, or why should every cottage have had a rowan without fail? Indeed, most of the ruins boast of two protectors from evil spirits and witches; and the clachan beside Inchtomach goes by the eerie name of Boglechynack.

I have heard that it was here, long ago, that there lived a Howdie-wife who was disturbed one night by a knocking at her cottage door. Peering into the dusk (for the sun had dropped behind Meall Buachaille as if the Shepherd had swallowed it at one gulp), she saw a lady wrapt in a pale green plaid. The visitor requested her services for a friend. The Midwife felt strange about going, for there was something queer about the visitor, and who could want her? Did she not know every soul within a distance of many miles? However, a call was a call, even though it led up the water of Nethy to a faerie mound!

Of the appearance of the interior of the magic place, of the people whom she assisted, or the faerie baby that was born, the nurse retained no recollection. The lady accompanied her back to the cottage, and was seen by the husband, who by this time had returned from his work. The Howdie was asked what she would like as a reward for her services and asked for success at her profession; and though she left the glen shortly after her strange experience, her wish was not only granted for herself, but applied also to the following generations, who worked for many years in another district and handed down the wonderful reputation.

I followed the path as it winds past the memorial to Maxwell " Who loved to roam these hills," and over a little bridge to where a mound lies surrounded by bog, with only dead trees standing like ghosts among the purple fire of its heather. I lay on the rise, taking my view through the miracle of its myriad blossoms. To the right a run of dark green firs sloped to the gully below. Over the tops of the trees the land lay folded like some exquisite drapery ; a turn sharp as a sudden corner of stiff brocade where the shoulder of Meall Buachaille shelters the deserted croft of Rebhoan, and another as soft as satin where the green side of Ruig da ros, the hill of the two views, drops to the defile which hides the Green Loch.

The Nethy glinted here and there among the foot-hills ; foot-hills that would have loomed large had it not been for the overlording background—the rolling curves of Mam Suim, and Bynack Beag and the bold side of the corrie that leads to Loch A'an. Behind them, beyond them, rose the top of A' Charn Gorm itself, capped with a silver helmet of snow.

Having adjusted one's eye to see the great scaurs as if one scaled their intimacies, having swung among distant precipice and corrie, a sudden drop of the viewpoint shows the trees of the glen below, so tiny as to be ridiculous, shows them as playthings too small to finger—and yet, the height of them above the tallest stalk of heather !

I have flown only once, and that was in the days when aeroplanes resembled hair-nets rather than 'buses with wings, but I felt the same buoyant sensation on gazing that day through those miles and miles of uninterrupted air to the heights of the hills and back to the heather-bells that brushed my

face. Then, like a blow, the extraordinary un-
consciousness of nature seemed suddenly terrible.
The blossom that cannot move and does not know
its neighbour. The hill that cannot see, that has no
voice and does not know its name. It was a moment
equivalent to the ghastly second that comes to Youth
when it suddenly throws off sentiment and sees its
parents as no more than normal man and woman;
but just as such cold reasoning is followed by a
sudden excess of affection, as if through the father
and mother all past generations clamoured to be
recognised, so the heather scent became one with
my breath, the song of the river was my song, the
trees my playmates under the eyes of the serious big-
brother hills. I took the track down to the Green
Loch so permeated with the scene that I was not
aware of putting one foot before the other.

A green loch might well be green with snow
water or green with weed; but this particular
Lochan Uaine that lies between Glenmore and
Abernethy is of a green unbelievable. The colour
is emerald tinged with blue and as clear as glass. It
may be due to the presence of bitumen or some other
chemical, but you need know nothing of chemistry,
for plenty of Speyside folk will give you the reason.
They will tell you that on nights of the full moon
strange figures flit to and fro on the high slopes, and
with silvery laughter that is stolen by the wind at its
first sound, the faerie folk come down to the little
loch and rinse their green robes in the clear water,
leaving the stain of the magic green dye. If you
should disturb them you would probably be blinded
or maddened by seeing for ever in your mind little

crescents of silver that come and go ; crescents that might be the gleam of the moon on a faerie shoulder unprotected by its sheath of green raiment, but crescents that would always melt into the black pool of your mind as a ripple dies in the stillness of a loch.

Between Rebhoan (now used as a bothy) and the loch, once lived an old man with the gift of improving eyesight. He was a woman-hater, and lived alone. One day, a woman by name MacQueen, suffering from sore eyes, decided to risk asking his help. He gave her a charm, but as he truly threatened, it was one that she would not forget. Only three lines of it there were, but—they left her as blind as a stone for the rest of her life.[1]

Here it was also that a farm hand, not so long ago, returning at night on his way from Abernethy to Glenmore, heard the faerie pipes. Sceptical at first, but obliged to believe his ears, he was staggered at the thought of returning so long a road, but could not rid his mind of the risk of disappearing for seven years if the Daoine Sith should invite him. On tiptoe he crept forward, his mind wrestling with some plan to please the Good-folk and win their favour. The sound of the pipes rose and fell and rose again to die away as if he had been suddenly seen through the blackness of the night. He decided to make a dash for it, and had just started to run when the pipes began again in full blast, and turning his head in spite of the risk of looking, he saw a Tinkler's fire dimly smouldering. All the rest of the camp were trying to sleep, and maybe managing it, but the

[1] *In the Shadow of Cairngorm*, Dr. Forsyth.

restless spirit of the piper urged him to send his cry to the lonely hills.

It has surprised me to find that Tinklers are not singing folk. Some of them play the pipes, but few of them play really well, and their voices are usually harsh. Nor are they believers in the Faerie faith, though some of them will admit having seen a tannasg, a ghost of some person dead a hundred years maybe, and one woman assured me that her dead cat went with her still, and often arrived in camp before them. Some of the older women can hear Death on the wind before he visits the tents, and one such told me that "the dead are very cold as they pass you by." Most of the Tinklers are anxious for their dead to lie in hallowed ground, and no graves are more carefully tended or more ornamented with the " flowers that die not " and with messages of peace than are the graves of the Tinklers in the Kirkyairds.

One feels sorry for the hardships of the Tinklers, though of course they are inured to it from their youth; and even if their troubles are largely due to themselves, it is impossible on closer acquaintance not to respect the people to whom the call of the road is as loud and distinct as the cry of the curlew, and who respond to it without the need for words, just as the wild swans wing unprotesting across the wide silence of the night.

THE VANISHED VILLAGE

The Pass of the Sluggan lies between Pityoulish on the Spey and the Glenmore forest. Lovely as is the winding road along the deep gully lined with dark trees, the interest is concentrated at the northern end where the track opens on to the strath at Kincardine and is bordered on one side by an ancient burial-ground and on the other by a village that has not quite finished disappearing into the hillside on which it once stood in obvious array.

The outline of cottage after cottage to the clear number of seventeen is visible among the great blocks of rock ; otherwise the brae is barren except for a gnarled gean tree that raises its twisted branches in spring pride and spills the silver tears of its flourish on to the close turf.

Here one day an old acquaintance joined me in the silence that belongs to this deserted side of the river. To know a tale of the past oneself is good ; to hear it repeated by one whose days penetrate into the past three times as far as one's own is better.

" In the old, the brave strong days that used to be," he said, giving the word " strong " an emphasis accompanied with a vigorous dig of his stick into the grass, " these ruins were the houses of the bhaile of Kincardine, where lived the Barons of

Kincardine who were Stewarts and descendants of King Robert II. They possessed all the land hereabouts. I have counted nigh on twenty foundations of houses here, and of their bonny gardens there is only that old gean tree still standing, though I mind many more of them and apple trees too in my younger days. But the brave days are gone, and the last Baron of Kincardine is buried in the Cladh yonder. He sold the Barony for a handful, having been in some mischief I doubt."

He paused, straightening himself as his eye roved

THE OLD GEAN TREE

up the shadowed pass and away to the spread of sunlit strath, opening his eyes wide as if he saw also, and without the slightest difficulty, the spread of the years that lay here before the day of his birth.

"There would have been raids before that and after that," he added, "and you may be sure that treasure will be buried in the neighbourhood, but who can tell where? Who would want it? Who would be so foolish as to seek it? Who can tell where?" he repeated as he went down the braeside, the white of his beard catching the glint of the sun, strength still in his step, and the fine pride in his heart. I felt ashamed of the paltry number of my years; but I too had my pride of race, even though a cuckoo sat in the gean tree and mocked the past, making queer noises to itself, unbecoming a feathered thing.

I climbed the hill behind the lost village, hoping with a hope that is ludicrous except on the spot, that I might find, not treasure, but some small intimate mark of the past, a metal pin, a ladle, anything that should break the gap of time and the awful stillness of a past people.

The cuckoo followed me, his cry now here now there, and fainter as the trees gave way to heather. I was glad that I had breakfasted, for it is not lucky to hear the call of the Faerie Bird before the fast of night is broken, even if the Natural History books have robbed him of his cosy winter quarters in some faerie hillock.

On the top of the hill opposite Culvardy Mill is an old fort. Just how ancient it is, no one will venture to say. The walls, built round a twenty-seven-foot circle, have been eleven feet in thickness; piled without mortar, one huge stone upon another, as children build—the children of giants.

I spent a summer's day in the heathery circle, with screaming gulls and a furry caterpillar for company. The range of the Cairngorm was hidden by the humped shoulder of Creag Ghreusaiche, and behind it also, to my advantage, was the East Wind. Far below, the waters of Loch Pityoulish were so clear that I could see the dark patch which is the sunken island and its castle; presumably a crannog or artificial isle of the Bronze Age whose foundation piles have sunk or collapsed. Visitors used to be warned that there was "Something" in the loch which made it unadvisable to put the head under water when bathing, for fear of spending the rest of life with "That" in the submerged castle. Perhaps the hidden piles have a connection with the caution without adding the harrowing tale of the lost lads of Pityoulish.

The young heir to the Barony of Kincardine was playing with some companions beside the loch, when they caught sight of a pony decked in wonderful saddlery, with silver bells on the reins and coloured bridle beset with jewels. The boys naturally seized the reins, and the creature immediately crashed into the water, taking every boy with him but the Baron's son, who had the presence of mind to feel for his sgian dubh and sever his fingers to free himself.

Even in the summer months the strath is spattered with lochs and pools: Loch Garten, Loch Mallachie, Loch Dallas, Loch Vaa, and Avielochan, besides several other smaller ones that lie with wide-open eyes to the huge expanse of sky. The Spey wriggles in curves, shadowed by the Monadhliaths in their plaid of dark-toned forest.

With a spy-glass I could have watched the deer descending to the shelter of the woods, but I can never bring myself to take "the long eye" with me on my rambles, it seems unfair and almost indecorous to pry from afar upon any creature whose instinct is satisfied of its privacy. As for my own privacy, I thought it ended when a large stone unexpectedly moved. The stone did not fall, it slid five inches on to one below, and the sound echoed and rumbled amongst the little cavities. Coincidence? Of course. Wild animal? Most probably; but the thought did not lessen the feeling that something was standing close behind me. Wholesome sunshine poured on to the hillside, drawing a faint scent of honey from the heather; the smoke of a train, like a wafted hen-feather, lay adrift in the valley. A normal world, one would have said; but the hilltop was wide, and the silence numbing. With no human nearer than the depth of a sea away, discomfort seized me, and I took the short-cut down that is good for the saving of time, but bad, very bad, for the clothes.

Some weeks later I mentioned the fort to a man who was busy at work in a byre.

"Creag a' Chaisteil?" he echoed. "It is a place not to linger. The Raiders had it. A wild people. They say silly things about it. I do not believe them." I looked at him and said nothing, because I did not feel quite safe to join in the ridicule.

The Church of Kincardine is just a little grey-and-white sister to all the other Speyside Churches. In the fifteenth century it had a theekit roof; a roof which proved the undoing of the Comyns, who seem to have been unlucky in Churches.

During a visit to the Baron of Kincardine the Comyns murdered the Laird of Grant, who was also a guest. This breach of good manners must have been an unpremeditated deed, the result of a sudden flame of anger, for the sin was unforgivable and the visiting Comyns were too small a band to defend themselves. The dead being dead, there was no

time for argument, and the guilty did not stop to try
it; they quickly showed the soles of their hairy
curan, though they did not have the chance to
flee far before the combined Stewarts and Grants
were on their heels, and their only hope of refuge
was the sanctuary of the Church. Into this they
rushed, knowing as the door slammed and the bar

KINCARDINE CHURCH

fell that the pursuers dared not touch them within
the quiet walls of the holy edifice. The thought
was only momentary comfort, for they had no
food, nor could a messenger be sent to get relief,
whereas the Grants had doubtless despatched a
runner to Freuchie for reinforcements, and the
siege was thus likely to last until starvation claimed
the victory.

Such patient tactics, however, did not suit the
Grants or the Stewarts. Immediate revenge was

their burning desire.   Burning is the right word
to use, for they conceived the idea of shooting a
blazing arrow into the thatch.   The missile rose
slowly and fell, striking the rushes without sound,
and silence fell on the attackers as a little scarlet line
ran along the ridge where the thatch was driest.

With what horror the prisoners must have looked
upon the first thin trail of smoke among the rafters ;
foreseeing their own fate in the sight of the gasping
warrior who first felt the oppression of its stifling
thickness on his lungs ;   hearing the crackle of
sparks, then the roar of blazing timber, cries and
curses mixed with prayer, the groans of dying men
silenced by the crashing of falling masonry.   Hell
for an hour before Hell was due !

One Comyn alone made a dash for the door in the
hope of escape, but he was cut down, and the Grants
and the Stewarts continued to watch the burning
with the fierce glee of the avenger, while their
womenfolk and children watched from the little
houses on the brae, satisfied that all was being done
that could be done to retrieve the honour of the
Clan whose guest lay dead upon the host's table.

Pityoulish and its Kirk offer many an interesting
puzzle.   The Church is situated on a mound with
a track that indicates the former presence of Druids.
A green sea of flat field surrounds the hillock, and
a sacred well and a dew-cup which has never been
known to be dry, indicate further proof that this
place found favour with the Priests of Skill.

The well, which has been filled in, because the
accidental sacrifice of lamb was too frequent an
occurrence, was called the Well of Tomhaldidh.

MUCKRACH CASTLE

(page 149)

The name offers a thousand possibilities, but the
Mound of Allaidh—a Wolf—seems the most
natural guess, since the very last wolf of the North
was killed near here, as it was in so many other
places !

I felt resentful on first learning that the Church
was dedicated to St. George. What was Merrie
England and its Dragon doing up here ? Then I
remembered that St. George was indeed far from
home, being a native of Syria, but he has at least
another, both saintly and foreign, to keep him
company, for St. Catherine of Alexandria shares
the honour of the Church with him. It may be that
his dragon links with many a Celtic monster, and
even with the Byzantine-looking creatures on ancient
sculptured stones in the vicinity, while Catherine's
wheel of fire is also a solar emblem, and was probably
in use on this mound long before Christian Mission-
aries brought new threads of thought to interweave
with an earlier philosophy.

There is nothing in the Church now to accentuate
respect for either saint. The last restoration, some
time about 1880, resulted in marked changes. The
western door was moved to its present position at
the side, and not till I was obliged to tread on tombstones to unlock the new door did I realise how
unreasonable it was of me to have tiptoed lightly
about the Cladh for fear of disturbing the dreams
of the dead ; for how should one escape them except
by aviation ? Further changes included the loss of
one of the two galleries and the blocking of the
leper's squint, which can now only be seen from the
outside, and there is no charm about a " keeking

hole " which no manner of squinting will enable one to see through.

Outside, where the ancient larch leans whispering to the bell, a dark stone marks the spot sacred to the memory of

WALTER STEWART
GRANDSON OF
ROBERT II. OF SCOTLAND

This Walter was the third natural son of the Wolf of Badenoch, and a gentler cub than the others ; not that that is saying much, though his father honoured him by disliking his more merciful mind.   If he did not inherit his Sire's taste for fire and murder, he held the finer Stewart code that his sword was brother to him, and was knighted for valiant work with it at the battle of Harlaw.

You will not find Lochaber marked here on the map, and yet a five-foot patch of this grass grows in Lochaber soil, for the daughter of Lochiel had expected that Death would end her exile and that then both she and her dowry would be taken back to the west, but the Baron of Kincardine had no such expensive notions with regard to his wife's funeral, and a few creels of Lochaber turf fulfilled the letter of her request.   As for the dowry, it would go into neither wallet nor kist, for it consisted of a dozen black-haired Lochaber lads for the lady's protection and service.

The field surrounding the Church joins the madder-tinted hills on one side, and spreads down to the Manse and across to the farm of Auchgourish. It is a stretch of quietness where even the low-voiced discontent of a calf sounds like sudden thunder and the toppling cry of the peesweep hurts the air ; and yet, once a year this little plain used to seethe with people. Folk in holiday attire, Lairds and their ladies, crofters and byre-lassies, henwives with fluffy stock screeching from their arm-pits, spae-wives and jugglers, pipers, dancers, pedlars of fairings, men with wool and women with web, jostled and shouted like the waves of a spring tide that run merrily over unaccustomed grass.

The tide has receded and left no sound nor sign of the Figgat Fair. " The Needle Fair " my old friend called it, for there the women purchased their knitting-needles and sold the work of their hands, " Fighe " being a word relative to the arts of weaving and knitting. The date of the Fair was the first of June, which in Old Style represents the twentieth of May and gives the name " Fichead," twenty (pronounced " fich-ut ").

No wonder St. George's popularity faded in Abernethy, for this countryside had a local hero to supersede him. John Roy Stewart was a native of Kincardine, a singer, a fearless fighter, a piper, and a friend of the Prince in whose defence he won high praise from the enemy at Culloden.

This cheerful man with the red hair and small hands was exiled for his loyalty, and roved the Abernethy hills composing psalms to suit his own conditions, such as—

> " The Lord 's my targe, I will be stout
>   With dirk and trusty blade,
>   Though Campbells come in flocks about
>   I will not be afraid.

" The Lord 's the same as heretofore,
    He 's always good to me ;
Though redcoats come a thousand more,
    Afraid I will not be."

Give his deeds of kindness, his acts of valour, a
few more years on the lips of the people, and John
Roy Stewart may join Wallace and Bruce in the
hero-march towards the land where Fionn and
Arthur, Cuchulainn and Bran sit among the gods,
beckoning modern boyhood from the stucco path
of mediocrity.

Old Mary Stewart, said by some to be a descendant of John Roy, is still remembered as she
was so often seen, passing up and down the Sluggan
with her little cart. What was in it ? Peat or
kindling by the look of it ; but appearances can be
deceptive, as the gaugers knew. Fortunately for
Mary they knew something more than her brewing
of " the precious "—they knew the taste of it. She
would give them a tassie in her cottage, and such
was the magic of the potion that a man would forget
where he had tasted it, until such a time as he was
ready for some more. Perhaps it was Mary's
bothy that John Hill Burton describes as situated in
Glenmore and " made of bent roots of pine-tree
found in the neighbouring mosses and covered with
turf. It was so low that a traveller might have
walked over it without observing that it was an
edifice made by human hands."

Between the road and the east end of Loch Pityoulish (or Bhaileyoulish as the natives politely call
it) lies a hollow where the heather will not grow,
nor juniper nor grass nor any other plant than the

blaeberry; for here the Shaws annihilated a party of Comyns, thanks to the help of an old woman upon the Callert hill who gave the Shaws the signal to attack at the right moment. Not one Comyn was left, and since then no plant will grow in the gruesome hollow of their graves except the plant of the Comyn Clan, the blaeberry.

I did not need to ask the surname of the one who was the recounter of that event, for the eyes glinted and the voice was as the sound of a dirk rattling on the hard hollow of a targe.

ACROSS THE STREAM

OPPOSITE the Church of Kincardine, the Castle of Kinchurdy used to frown across the river from its high mound. The farm which has taken its place seems to run upstream in contradiction to the swiftly running water, and the sturdy boat moored to the shore looks like a stranded green leaf.

Below the mound in summer time, the walled-in space is a mass of colour : scarlet and gold, crimson and blue, as if the Sun-god had tried his hand on a small square of Bâtik, dividing the radiant colours of his rays in an orgy of patterned loveliness. Beside the farm lies a long, low cottage, puzzling in its composition of rough stone and timber. This used to be a creel house and holds the title of the oldest domestic building on Speyside. In 1777 a timber frame rose, as now, from the stone base, but its walls were double-cased with wattling two feet apart, which was filled in with turf. In length as now, but with even lower heather-thatched roof pierced by a hole to let the smoke out but minus a window to let the light in, it must have been very like a cave ; and yet in the sixteenth century, not only the peasants, but the smaller landowners were content with such homes.

Sir Thomas Dick Lauder wrote of Gibbon Mhor as residing at Kinchurdy, but the great Cumming lived farther down the river near Boat of Garten in a Castle similarly situated, but of which nothing is now left except buried foundations and an outline of the moat.

Cummin Gibbon Mhor of Kinveachy and Glencarnie and of this Castle of Pitlac was such a force in Strathspey in the early fifteenth century that only those who could claim clanship felt safe from pillage, fire, or sudden death. The Cummin was ready to accept more followers for purposes of further intimidation, and was willing to receive persons into the Clan to bear his name and incidentally to defend his authority. The aspirants had to submit to baptism in a trough from which the hens drank; Gibbon being big enough to take his new full-grown children by the feet and dip them head first into the unclean water, after which befoulment they were known as Cummich Clach nan Cearc, the Cummings of the Hen Stone.

The trough is said to be the stone that leans against the Church of Duthil, but even though Gibbon's daughter is credited with founding that Church, it hardly seems likely that so great a stone would be carried all those miles over the hills without reason sufficient in importance to have been remembered.

This daughter Matilda or Bigla was something of a character, and has taken on legendary proportions as the gathering dust of years dims reality. Her smallest acts have become tales, and various stones in the vicinity are connected with her movements. Her angling methods were of the variety that approved of obtaining the biggest catch with the least waste of time; which is apparently an inconceivable outlook to modern sportsmen, who seem to rejoice in the reverse process.

Bigla contrived by means of a net in the salmon pool below the Castle, that the fish should announce themselves when caught, and should also simultaneously announce one item on the menu for the day. Movement in the net dragged on a cord which pulled a bell in the kitchen quarters. One can almost hear a disgruntled gillie shout to his boy, " The bell again ! Is that a visitor at the front port or a fish at the back ? "

On the wooded side of Drumullie hill lies a stone which is cited as the " cashie " for Pitlac Castle keys on the occasions of Matilda's churchgoing. This variant of The Key under the Mat or Above the Door is not very credible, since the hole is only four inches in diameter and keys in those days were levers and too large for even generous pouches, or if they were small enough to fit such a hole, why should Bigla have bothered to deposit them ? Sir Arthur Mitchell suggests that the stone was used by the early Scandinavian invaders as an oath stone, though he does not claim for those people the myriad cairns that are dotted among these woods.[1]

One of the largest cairns, which used to be known as Tom Tigh an Leigh, the House of the Hill Doctor, is said to have been raised by the parents of illegitimate children, who were obliged to place a stone for each child. The cairn is partly tumbled now, but counting the stones that are still piled and those that are fallen, the number runs to hundreds !

[1] *Vacation Notes in Strathspey*, Arthur Mitchell.

The tale is obviously a gathered one, by the number of similar cairns in the vicinity, and also from the fact that this was known to be the Warriors' Burial Ground of a prehistoric people, the old name being Glen a Ceatharnach, the Glen of the Heroes.

Battle carnage brings birds of prey, and the adjoining hill is named after the Ravens (Creag Fhitich), so Duthil Parish must be considered clear of scandal. The best of our cenotaphs, crosses, and sculpture cannot vie with the old cairns as war memorials. Before battle every man placed his stone to the heap. After the battle, those who were able, took away a stone, and there was left a "count" of the dead who had thus raised their own monument. What is a pillar of masonry and lime raised two or three years after a war, compared with such an intimate reminder set as a last act by the hands of the dead?

From the eastward slopes of these hills that divide the Dulnan from the Spey, the wide strath stretches in colour and texture of homespun, with green pattern-pieces of satin oats and velvet pasture flung down on the heather beside toy farms. Hidden by the double line of the railway lies Tullochgorm; a place of importance before Time and other enemies had flung its greatness astray. It is connected with Bigla in that her second son was Patrick MacIan Roy, the ancestor of the Clan Phadruig Grant of Tullochgorm. When the old mansion was destroyed, the household spirit left the place. This spirit was no vague apparition, but a gruagach or family guardian. The Gaelic term implies the possession of a superabundant head of hair, which was the outstanding feature of such spirits, but the supernatural housekeeper of Tullochgorm had in addition a paw or hairy hand and was therefore known as the Mag Mulloch.

It sounds rather a disagreeable defect, but a great deal could be overlooked in one who acted as a domestic and who gave faithful and unrequited service year after year as Lairds came and went. The Mag Mulloch floated through the air to attend at table, and superintended the work of the dairy. Nor did it scorn less usual duties, among them the safe conduct of its Master at night when he had been from home and in convivial company. On such occasions it was considerate enough of his feelings to simulate the appearance of a small boy carrying a candle for guidance along the moorland path. The head of the house was evidently its special care, and the Goodwife was chased to bed in terror of the Mag Mulloch's grimaces when the Laird wished to remain below-stairs to entertain his cronies alone.

The term " gruagach " for the Highland household goddess is interesting in its possible relationship to the word " groac'h," which was the name given to the Druidic Priestesses of Brittany whose duty was to re-thatch the Temple every year.

Tullochgorm lies about two miles from Boat of Garten, which is a queer little place, built anyhow, marred by the railway and seeming still to resent the bridge across the river in the place of the old " Penny over " chain ferry. On the road between " the Boat " and Aviemore lies the estate of Kinveachy, and I will repeat the story of its Bonnet Stane as it was told to me.

"It was Ian lay panting on the side of the hill beside the dead stag. Maybe he had a right to it—maybe, and maybe not. The gralloch finished, the question to him was how to get the venison home without being seen. That must evidently be the way of 'A lion beag is bheagan, mar a dh'ith an cat ant-iasg' (little by little as the cat ate the fish). So he set to work and cut, and not being able to carry all the pieces, he hid two legs of the beast in the sandy bed of a pool in the near-by stream. When he was gone, along came Colin Grant seeking a strayed foal and with an eye for such folk as that Ian. He found the little creature of a foal lying crushed to death below a fallen boulder. Colin skinned it and went down to the pool to clean his hands, and hadn't the water washed the venison clear to the eye! So Colin smiled, and back he went to the foal and cut two legs off it and set them in the pool in the place of the venison, and away home he went. Next black night, back came Ian very softly and all, and took the meat from the stream. Whether he saw by the light of his candle when he got home, or whether he did not know till discomfort told him—anyway, he found the deceit and his knife itched for bigger sport than deer stalking.

"That was the way Ian and Colin met, and it would be death for one of them, and it is not too long ago that something of the kind happened in a place that I know of—but—in this tale now, Ian's sgian dubh was the tricky one and shhh-ht! Ah! Colin was no more for the watching. Ian buried him too deeply to be found, but set the dead man's bonnet a-scrog on a tall standing stone to tell the tale . . . and that 's the story of the Bonnet Stane of Kinveachy."

The Bonnet Stone or Clach nam Bonnach is a term that has come down unchanged through the oldest tales, and it is of particular interest that a version should have been revived to fit a local story in a district peculiarly rich in stone circles. For versions of the original tale mostly concern a wicked giant who carefully secrets his soul in a stone and thus cannot be killed by his earthly enemies. The heroine searches for it, making excuse that she wishes to do the soul honour. "It is in the Clach nam Bonnach," says the villain. The heroine then follows the custom of dressing the bonnet stone with clothing and ornament, and professes to pay homage to it; only to find that the wicked one has removed his soul elsewhere. This serious game of "hunt the soul" continues according to the inventive powers of the teller, but the soul is eventually found in an egg which the hero or heroine crushes, and in so doing kills the villain.

Nor is this story peculiar to the Highlands alone, it is contained in the folk tales of other countries, the Russian version being very similar in detail.

Between Kinveachy and the wild duck haunt of Avinlochan, a bank beside the road is decorated with a tracery of paths that lead skyward. It is almost impossible to imagine anything but the land of the Sun lying beyond the sudden arrest of those heather tracks. In spite of this impossible anticipation there is no disappointment in the sudden view of

Loch Vaa.   Its little bays of shallow water are inset
northward in forest land, and reed-edged pools, like
individual lochans, reveal their inmost secrets through
the clear water.   In spite of its nearness to the Carr
Bridge route, Loch Vaa preserves its remoteness and
holds inviolate its relationship with Wind and Sun.

BY THE WITCHES' HUTS

THERE is a restfulness, a happy content in expected beauty, but a sudden unanticipated loveliness flings one's heart into the air.

That is what happens at Carr Bridge where a sudden leaping span of stone, thin as a crescent moon, is thrown over the river. It rises on the one side from an outjutting rock, and without buttress or embellishment leaps high over the brawling Dulnan.

It is not unlike the Old Roman Bridge of Lanark, and I know of only one other span that exactly resembles it, which is in Italy, so one may surely give the credit to the Romans. To the left the road branches away through Slochd Muick, where, as indicated by the name, wild boars used to harass the inhabitants. According to records, bands of thieves overcame the swine and carried on the work of plunder. The gentry journeying by coach to take part in the gaieties of the Northern capital took breath at Carr Bridge and did not relax again until the stretch of dark moor and mountain gave place to the lower levels of Strath Dearn. Even in the nineteenth century the barefaced robberies continued, and a bride of Rothiemurchus had the trunk containing her entire trousseau cut away from the back of the coach in which she was travelling with escort to Inverness.

Beside the bridge a track leads on to the Monadh-liath range, the subdued opposing partner of the Monadh Ruadh mountains. There is nothing dramatic in the form of these hills, they fold on to a high plateau in a manner more lovable than striking, but their pine-glades run like amazing opera settings. Tree trunks and more tree trunks; half a mile of trees, a mile or two miles of needled path enclosed from the sky by heavy foliage, and the view ever the same, six, or two hundred and sixty feet away. Nothing but trees and impossible rocks, seemingly made of *papier mâché* that rise from the brown ground with unbelievable fungi relieving the sombre colour.

I used to think that artists' brains were the only spawning-grounds of scarlet faerie houses spotted white, of yellow helmets and minute frilled parasols; but I have seen just such things actually growing in the Monadhliath woods. Not only these, but also huge ochre cups concave to the sky, filled with blood-red wine to overspilling, so that I half expected to hear the cry, " Awake, ye Bacchanals. Hear the sound of hornéd kine. Awake ye ! " But the only sound that breaks the silence is the tired and comfortable plaint of the cushat, fussing with her untidy nest. It will always be untidy, for when the magpie was sent to teach all the birds how to build, and proposed that sticks be taken one at a time and set criss-cross, the woodpigeon had an idea of her own. " Take two-oo," she suggested, " take two-ooo," and persisted in her reckless policy till the magpie left her to it in disgust.

It is about four miles up the river from Carr

Bridge to Dalnahaitnach, a walk which can be taken up one side of the Dulnan and down the other. "There comes no salmon in this water," says MacFarlane," but extraordinary much kipper, that is salmon in the forbidden time. Gentlemen can kill 160 in a night. They used to feast the Sheriff to escape the fine."

Dalnahaitnach brings to mind the doings of one Ian Beag MacAndrea, for his little home was here and he was in it on a day when a party of well-armed men came to revenge the death of a comrade. It was one of those affairs when every one is in the wrong, for the deceased had been killed by Ian for stealing some one else's cattle to eke out his own marriage feast. However that may have been, it was undeniably awkward that eight men should arrive where Ian was sitting at his own fireside.

"Is it Ian Beag you are wanting?" asked his wife with unconcern. "He's up the brae with the cattle, I'll send the Herd for him." Turning to Ian she dealt him a good clout on the side of the head (for which no doubt she would need to answer later) and bid the lazy good-for-nothing seek his master. After partaking of a hurried meal provided by the wife, the impatient visitors filed out of the door one by one, and one by one they silently entered the narrower little black door of Death, for Ian was aloft in a pine tree beside the house, and his swift arrows pinned each man as he came with the sureness of an entomotomist. The bodies were buried down by the river, as you may yet see.

The way back to Inverlaidnan hill is mostly of General Wade's making as part of the original

CASTLE ROY

(page 156)

Inverness highway. It crosses the railway to join
the Carr Bridge–Duthil road. That is its official
name, but for me it is The Road of the Unbelievable Rams. These mythic-looking beasts with
gigantic coils of horn balanced on their narrow heads
lie snorting under shadowed banks or stand stamping
their little black boots at the innocent traveller.

To the right the land slopes down to the old road
and rises again slowly to the fir-clad top of Creag
Fhitich which belongs to the Ravens. To the left
it leaps to high hills, and shows a gash in the
northern barrier known as Beum a Chla Chaidheimh,
the slash of the sword ; a weapon which must have
been half a mile in length to have cut such a pass,
and can only have been wielded by Fionn himself
at his greatest.

There are a few people who are clever enough to
live in the twentieth century without touching it ;
and the man who was busy in a peat hag had about
him a look of sheepskin and tartan. He held in
every turn of his tongue the dark essence of timeless
tragedy ; and he turned, with a phrase, the ancient
buried years, as his spade turned the time-pressed
peat to the light of day. Here was a man whose
friend had seen the witches at their work, and here
the very place where he had seen them ; in any case,
there is no reason to doubt the actual existence of the
hags whose little houses or huts have not long been
destroyed.

The friend was returning from one of the farms
that has created fruitfulness at an incredibly high
altitude in these barren hills. The evening was
still, dropping swiftly to darkness, the only sound

was the occasional chuckle of the grouse, the only light a sky reflection from the lost sun. As he came towards a dip that faces the road below Lyndeor, he heard the sound of the pipes, and expecting to see some of his friends, he hurried to the hollow. At the edge of it, a sudden fierce wind flapped the tails of his coat, a strange light illuminated the upper part of his face, and peering downwards he saw a sight that made his skin creep like a living thing ! Four witches he saw, two of them dancing wildly, their eildrich shrieks piercing above the mad music, the shadows of their skinny bare arms seeming to add elongated limbs to their bent bodies. The two at the pipes were in league with the Wind himself, and the tune was one to rend the very soul from the body. The man fell on his knees, but being too flustered to remember a prayer, he used them for crawling away from the unnatural scene. When the normal use of his legs came back to him, he made a three-mile circuit round the far fir wood rather than take the short half-mile cut near the hollow to his home.

It is two and a half miles up the wild road to Garrocher where, under the shadow of Creag na h Iolaire, are the broken walls of the witches' cottages. Beside them is the humped ruin of a kiln, behind them the hill rises abruptly. The foreground, except for the blessing of a group of rowans, is a scene of raw fissures, as if an absent-minded god had begun operations with a porridge spurtle and had been called away before his plans were recognisable. All the middle distance consists of running hills—down and far, far and farther, till it seems as if the eye has travelled the length of all Scotland before the view is cut off by the frail blue curtains of the Cairngorm mountains looped to the sky.

I have not mentioned the shooting-rest, as, not being built of stone, it does not fit in with the scene. I buried a discarded cigarette-box with angry energy, and regretted that I could not bury the shooting-rest also. The Witches' Well near-by has been gifted with many a pebble, and I even saw two pins, both very rusty, in its shining water. I added a pebble myself with a carefully considered wish. Just as well that I was cautious, for I heard later that " There 's not a wish at that same Well but that it comes true." One may call it wishing, but the difference between a wish and a prayer is only the lack of a definite medium, and I pondered over my pebble gift as I wound my way down the rough track, consoling myself with the thought that I was not alone in my guilt, for no less than £21 was taken from Tobar na Coille at Culloden in 1927!

In Duthil itself, that place of " vertuous women of olden days who yearly enriched their husbands with money by the making of cloth," lived the famous Wizard, Willox. A strange man he was : clever, shrewd, a juggler and amateur scientist, who earned his living by hoaxing a public that was quite willing to pay for its illusions. He is mostly spoken of now as " That bad man Willox," and certainly he was not too scrupulous in his methods, for mysterious diseases among cattle that were prevalent in his lifetime, and could only be cured by him at high charges, ceased to bother the creatures after his death. He had some veterinary and medical knowledge, and however guiltlessly he had applied it, he would have been accused by the people of his day of witchcraft.   Although as smart as Sherlock Holmes in his intricate methods of tracing thieves and criminals, there were occasions when his brain and luck failed him, and he died discredited by many, having done more by his few failures to put an end to superstition than all the rigorous mandates of the Church.

Before the day of Willox, the Saint's Well of Duthil, which lay between the present Manse and the Church, was the scene of a strange vision.

A man from Clury came to the well one day and was astonished to see by the side of the holy water, a fire blazing under a great brazen cauldron.   The cauldron was filled with the white beauty of snow-buntings, and round it stood the souls of unbaptized children robed in white.   The man was seized with the desire to own the pot.   Twice he pleaded in vain, and on the third request was told that he might take it, but with the curse upon him that " There would not stand in the gathering of Strathspey but one bonnet for three generations of those who should come after him."

The curse took its course, but what became of the precious pot is not known.   After that event, Clury was said to be an unlucky spot, and one who lived there has hinted to me of some restless spirit— of a window seen lighted when no one was in the house—it may be that Alan Mor is correcting his accounts.

Perhaps the story of the Cauldron of Duthil is a memory survival of Druidic rites which included the

sacred fire and the birds of augury. The man who
desired the Cauldron was not an initiate, and the
contents were poison to all save the instructed, so
that while its contents were ordinarily productive of
fertility, to the insistent man of Clury it brought the
curse of lack of progeny.

A different kind of ill-will upset the village for
many years, making the pulpit of Duthil Church a
difficult charge to fill. The congregation had its
own way of expressing disapproval; cats in the
Manse Well being the mildest form of protest. The
trouble had commenced with an overheard remark
of the Minister's at a christening, to the effect that
" another demon had been added to the tribe."
The offended father took reprisals, with the result
that the Minister wished that the parish might be
deprived of Ministers till the seventh generation.
His wish is outlived long ago.

The Church is new and rather overshadowed by
the family vault of the house of Grant. A bronze
plate on the tall studded door of this little castle of
Death is inscribed with the names of Earls and
Countesses, Knights and Ladies, persons once gay
or grave who lie within. The door will never be
opened again, for the last lines read :—

" In terms of the Testamentary writings of Caroline
Stewart, Countess Dowager of Seafield, this Mausoleum
has been closed and is not to be used for further inter-
ment."

Not far from the last resting-place of the Earls of
Seafield rises the gaunt ruin of Muckrach Castle.
The lands of Muckrach were given to the Grants in

1570, and twenty-eight years later the tower was built by Patrick Grant, with the motto over the main door, "In god is al my traist." A fitting statement from one who had a further gift of the lands of Rothiemurchus. Patrick found the later gift somewhat difficult to keep from the outlawed Shaws who laid claim to it, and therefore he deserted this lordly pile that still lifts its multi-coloured stones in turreted pride, and went to live beside his newly acquired forest. At that time Muckrach had vaulted basements, a watch-tower, courtyard, and out-buildings. It is a portion of the main tower that still stands, with the corkscrew stair that used to lead to two upper floors and an attic, but which now leads unhindered to the sky. The broken roof of the vaulted basement opens just beside this stair, but a better way to enter is by the low door that leads from the outside of the building. All unsuspecting, I sought the shelter of this wine-cellar on a day of driving sleet, and was so amazed at the result of my entrance that I really hardly knew what happened. One moment I was alone in the white light of the sleet, and the next I was in the middle of the earth fighting a host of devils! The air was full of flying hoofs as a herd of small ponies scrambled up to the door, jammed each other, and at last stampeded clear of the improvised stable, which is quite a fitting place for those whose future work will be in the darkness of coal pits.

The road to Dulnan Bridge walks beside the running river whose water is as black as a Tinkler's brew, with foam riding white among amber tints. I cannot understand how the Mill on the bank can

have ground more than a handful of meal at a time.
If, in its working days, the faeries used to make use
of it when the stone whorl was left off the spindle,
who could blame them?   It is such a charming, such
a very little mill, with a water-wheel not much more
than five feet in height, and a door that demands a
bowed head.   The building creeps to the water's

THE WEE MILL

edge as if afraid of the rampaging river.   It looks
also as if some former owner had shared its misgiving,
for the large rock that splits the torrent is adorned
with a model of a fish in iron, as if to appease the
water-spirit for the use of the stream.

The bridge by the Smiddy leads down Broomhill
—appropriately blazoned with broom in summer—
to the quietness of Abernethy; and the road straight-
on runs to Grantown.   No satisfactory conclusion
can be reached at cross-roads of such equal charm,
except by a severed worm, but for me the Grantown

way has a little added attraction because it passes Tom na Croich.

The little knoll is bare except for a very tall standing stone which was the predecessor of the Regality Cross of Grantown as the place of justice and often of dire punishment.   There was no appeal in the days of Heritable Jurisdiction.   The Chief hanged or beheaded as he thought fit on this spot where probably humanity had been sacrificed to other gods than Justice.   When he dealt out death to a widow's only son beside this grey pillar, she used the only weapon she had, and cursed him. " May your house never be without a fool ! " she cried ; which was a tag that relation or foe could use for all time as suited their convenience, but which might apply in its vague gradation to any family in the land.

It will probably have been proximity to the mote hill that gave the little pine wood its reputation of danger.   It is a " crow wood," and something less tangible, less desirable, than crows inhabits its shadowed aisles at night.   What exactly the nightly terror is or has been, is not told, beyond the fact that Something caused the death of a man by throwing him from his horse.

In the daytime it is a noisy wood, for crows are such untidy quarrelsome folk.   I find it hard to believe that there is such a thing as a hen-bird among them.   What is there of motherly fluffiness or feminine daintiness about a hard-beaked crow with its bedraggled shiny coat always lacking an important feather and possessing a voice like a broken klaxon horn ?   Only a young one that I found in this wood seemed fairly tidy, with a row of orderly white spots on its wing tips and with polished boot buttons for eyes. It was lying on the ground and seemed ill at ease and inclined to choke. I rendered what assistance I could, only to find that it had been sampling a diet of pine-needles and now wished to return them as unsuitable.

The path through the wood leads down to the Bailliefurth Ferry, where a boat is still obtainable if your lungs are good enough to make " Mach am bata " penetrate the house on the other bank, and you may safely pass over the river and join the road that runs to Abernethy; but here again you are among woods where the howlet unaccountably calls by day, where the uneasy dead have been known to disturb the deep hush of night, and giant death-candles flicker among the shadows.

THE BRAES O' ABERNETHY

ABERNETHY in the twelfth century was a very big parish under the see of the Bishop of Moray. The division ran as far east as Tomintoul, north to Cromdale, and south to Rothiemurchus, and yet the nearest gathering of houses to Abernethy Church is the comparatively new village of Nethybridge, whose store and station would fit without incongruity into a photograph of a South African dorp. Its Hotel would suit any small popular resort, its villas suggest the laboured respectability of suburbia, and the Nethy is spanned by a bridge so inconspicuous that one is not conscious of having crossed the water.

A bridge is the summer equivalent of a winter fireside. To lean over a high-sprung arch with the water running and singing among the stones below, is to feel the same sympathy of moving continuity, the same elation as is given by fire-flame. The bow of a bridge is a place to make new friends and keep old; a place to linger for a crack and add to one's philosophy. He who builds an uninspired bridge with high parapet and level span, cheats mankind of a summer vantage.

Half a mile beyond the river, Castle Roy stands on a knoll surveying the strath. It represents the oldest type of Scottish stronghold, the builders are named as the " Red Friers " or as the Comyns some time early in the thirteenth century. Its massive seven-foot walls enclose a large space, shadowed by the great height of the shell open to the sky. A division in the north-west corner shows where a square tower once reared its block to the winds, and the projecting stone ledge gives the feeling of the low roof that made comfort in its lowest storey.

The pointed doorway, eight feet in width, gapes across open country, and intimately reveals in its uneven stonework the difficulties and determination of the mason who, with no tools greater than his strong hands, and common sense, hung those stones between the earth and sky. Time and weather have made less useful breaches; and these give an uncomfortable feeling of insecurity, high and exposed as the building is to the miles of surrounding country. A wide niche in the northern wall suggests a fireplace, but there is little left to help the eye to reconstruction, even though the Castle was inhabited as late as the sixteenth century.

A vault once broke the level of the court, but, being dangerous to cattle, was filled up. It would surely have been more reasonable to keep the cattle from grazing inside the Castle! Perhaps the Abernethy people were afraid that the steps led down to the hidden treasure, as well as to the vault. I say "afraid," because the plague was said to be hidden with the treasure. Such a tradition suggests a burial-ground, and it is likely that the mound on which the Castle now stands was an ancient religious site, for local tales refer to it as sacred, and the dew-cup in the adjoining churchyard points to Druidical interest. Also the Friars imply the presence of a Monastery, perhaps later converted into the Castle.

If the Comyns had anything to do with it, the building has doubtless seen many a fight and murder, and an echo of savagery lurks yet under the walls, where numerous dens are untidy with half-eaten débris.   Stained bone of rabbit, variegated wing of chaffinch, show that the present Red Lord of the Red Castle dines at his pleasure ; and even the wild-rose trees that guard the eastern approach with thoughts of the Sleeping Beauty cannot dispel the adamant sternness of the ancient pile.

At the foot of Castle Roy stands Abernethy Church.   You can reach the building through a zig-zag wicket-gate, but the little house of God stands primly sealed.   It is difficult to connect this inhospitable attitude with the thought of a protecting Deity.   There is no person, however poor, in all this land who would deny shelter from a storm ; and yet these houses of prayer, where one may only pray on arranged occasions, are bolted and locked as if they expected no other visitor than the Devil himself.

One can therefore only roam among the wise dead, whose sad-faced memorials stand awry in the lush grass, as if the solemnity of Death is not incompatible with leaning an ear to a neighbour's tale. A quaint epitaph by a pessimist who was too tired to finish in rhyme runs :—

> " This stone erected and placed
>   here, does mark the Drear *abode* of those
>   who Once like us appeard.
>   Through life's Career they *trode*.

> Soon shall we like them be laid
> Beneath O grave thy turf
> Unconscious of all future age
> Mouldering away to dust."

Well, well, admittedly we all have our day, but near to this dirge a big dew-cup cheerfully reminds us that "It's dabbling in the dew makes the milkmaids fair," and also that the Druids were here before Christianity was known in Obair-neithich, whose river, the Nethy, is said to mean "God of Waters," and to refer to river worship.

If you climb the small knoll behind the actual village and past a sawmill, you come to the clachan of Lynstock. Just beyond the companionable gathering of its timber-covered cottages stands the Gallows Tree.

I have seen other trees that were used for the same gruesome purpose, but none have so depressed me as the Gallows Tree of Lynstock. The others all had some air of shame or distress ; they were ancient and withered or broken, but this great fir rears itself to the sky in splendour, as if it has thrived on the bodies tucked beneath its twisting roots, and its red bark has been nourished by the streams that ran from the nailed ears of the guilty. Not always the guilty either ! From its knotted arms men have hung and dangled in the wind for such mild offences as sheep-stealing and heather-burning, and Baillie Mor dealt out this death for no greater crime than disobliging him, while Baillie Roy hanged a man first and then set the jury to find him guilty !

The tree stands upon a sloping bank ; it seemed an ideal spot to eat my lunch, sheltered from the

wind and open to the sun, but somehow the food
choked me, and I went down by the river and found
a cranny washed out by winter waters. There I
made friends with a restless water-wagtail, who
after a good display of antics and a little stac-
cato conversation, settled at my elbow on her nest
of half-hatched eggs and by her company wiped
the unhappy memory of the Dule Tree from my
mind.

The Smiddy at Lynstock with its unconsciously
interesting conglomeration of old-fashioned tools
among the scrap-iron at the door, is a reminder that
between this spot and the Spey is the site of one of
the greatest enterprises ever tried in the Highlands.
It is always disappointing when a tale has no illustration, but all that was left of the gear of the smelting
furnaces of Balnagowan (the Smith's Village) has
been obliterated long since by the God of Waters.
The onslaughts of the river were not always cur-
tailed as they are now ; the present guarding struc-
tures look like wooden ships filled with boulders
and abut into the waters to turn the fury of the
stream.

In 1728 the York Building Company purchased
the timber of Abernethy forest for the purpose of
starting smelting furnaces. The natives must have
thought the Sasunnachs were either gods or madmen
when they explained that the ore to be smelted lay
fifteen miles away as the crow flies. The crow flies
a different way from the road a man must travel to
the hills of Lecht, across the mountains and through
rivers to beyond Tomintoul and back ; and the
distance by the shortest route must have been

twenty-two miles each way, with altitudes of one thousand seven hundred feet to be scaled and with snow lying a great part of the year.

However, the Company did not seem daunted by the prospect; they thought that with plenty of capital and lots of drink for the Highlanders they would soon start a paying industry. No fewer than a hundred and twenty horses were gathered to drag timber and bring ore in panniers from the mine. Each evening found the workers gathered round great bonfires, swilling free brandy; a bounty that did not have the intended amiable result, as it killed five men in one night!

The furnaces used charcoal for fuel and produced various iron implements and girders that were still to be seen in position in 1830; but the distance, the wild journeys, and the enormous amount of fuel needed, made the scheme too slow and costly, and if the Gaelic song be true the outbreak of a forest fire added to the loss and "Drove out the Sassunachs to seek the better English." So the Company suddenly decamped, leaving in exchange for the large debts that they had run up to the proprietors and the country—their useless gear, a few rough roads, a sawmill, and some rafts.

The roads and the rafts and the mill were legacies not to be despised. Up to the coming of the York Building Co., timber-floating, though only practised on a small scale, had been one of the most spectacular and dangerous of professions; for the timber had been guided down the swirling waters by men in curraghs—little hand-made boats of skin, so light that they could easily be carried on the back and could even more easily be capsized or crushed.

The York Company, under the management of that strange man Aaron Hill the poet, whose varied ventures always seemed to miss success, cleared a passage down the Spey and built stable rafts bound with chains, so that they could be guided by a couple of men with oars.   This system proved so successful that it was carried on continuously by others, and so swift was the descent from the mouth of the Nethy to Garmouth at the sea, that the Floaters leaving early in the morning were able to be back by night, returning on foot.

The forest of Abernethy has recovered from these onslaughts and stands dark and beautiful, a pride to the family and tenants of the house of Grant to whom it belongs.   The close connection between this Clan and its forest lands is illustrated by the coincidence of the storm which swept the district a few days after the death of the last direct heir.   Sir Ian was at the beginning of his career, and it seemed like a tribute from Nature that a young plantation of fir, from which the family badge is taken, should have been uprooted near the house by that storm, and the trees prostrated with their crowns all pointing to Castle Grant where the young Chief had so lately been cut down.

Thanks to Hull and York, the value of timber came to be recognised on Speyside, and small streams were soon commissioned for running rough logs to the mills.   For this purpose the sluice-gates of Loch an Eilein, Loch Morlich, and Loch Eanaich were always closed till the great waters had gathered the

MONDAY IN THE FOREST

(page 168)

rains and melting snows for the Spring Run, when the logs would be gathered at spots lower down the outlet burn.

On the morning of the run, a man would be sent to open the sluice-gates. A most enviable task. The darkness of early morning, the towering mountains peaked with snow, the deep black waters catching the first grey gleam of light, with only the wooden slats to hold back the tons and tons of aquatic weight. The slow turning of a wheel, the sound of grumbling chains, and a sudden spate of white—a roaring as of some angered thing that had overlong nursed its hate, and the surplus of the loch became a river, coursing madly down the bed of the denied burn, rolling great stones and leaping up unaccustomed banks, while far down the glen, on the edge of the forest, drowsy men drank an early dram and looked to the hooks on the tips of their larch poles while they listened for the sound of the coming water.

Beside them the piles of felled timber lay ready, and at the first onrush of waters, with shouting and laughter, and yells and commands, the trees were tumbled into the flood. Trunks that had known only the gentle benison of raindrops felt the first buoyancy of full water. A most unruly fleet; piling one upon the other at the least excuse, jamming on a cross-current, or heaving forty feet of timber into the air when an unsuspected rock barred the way, for all the world as if a kelpie played at tossing the cabar.

The Floaters ran along the bank as best they could; jumping crags and traversing hillocks, some-

times leaping into the torrent up to their thighs to
keep the mad masts going smoothly.   What wonder
that the task began with whisky, that whisky was
drunk at the mid-morning meal, and that its neat
warmth finished off the day?   Yet one hears no
complaints or records of insobriety.   When the logs
reached the Spey, they were under the care of other
men who made them into rafts for their journey
down the greater river.   There is no timber-rolling
now ;   carts and steam-waggons and the railway
connect the innermost recesses of the forest with the
outer world.

Up past the tree-covered beauty of Forest Lodge
a little path leads over the Nethy to Loch an Spoiraid.
The trees here are festooned with a lichen like trailing hair, as if an army of ancient men had torn
panic-stricken through the wood, leaving the most
of their grey beards entangled on the low boughs.
Huge ant-hills abound, the largest I have ever seen,
measuring four feet in height ; and, as everywhere,
the juniper, that mixture of whin and cypress,
flourishes on all sides.

The wood turns onto an open heath, scarred with
the dark of peat hags.   A derelict cottage with its
cover of nettles among the fallen stones views the
desolation, a rusty girdle with broken handle adding
to the tragedy of the lost roof.   There is no sign of
a loch on this upland, and yet, a few minutes' walk
brings you to the side of the Loch of the Spirit.
The tree stumps in the surrounding land suggest a
ghostly forest which must once have made dark the
shallow waters.

I was up there on a day of blustering wind and

sudden rain, and the gulls were cursing with enviable vehemence among the unfriendly elements.   In the disturbed water, gnarled tree roots raised their writhing tentacles, seeming indeed like ugly spirits acrawl on some sucking expedition among the surrounding bogs.

Most lochs as well as rivers were thought to be the abodes of malicious supernatural beings, and this half-hidden loch might well claim human victims in the black of night or even on misty days.

The hills were blanketed with grey cloud, and I willingly retraced my steps from this plateau on the edge of nothing, back to the Lodge and westward towards Carn Rynettin in search of a spring that is known as the Boiling Well.   The thought of it seemed good as the wind bit on hands already numb with the cold of rain.   Dr. Forsyth refers to this well as " geyser "; [1] and for fear that intimacy with bathroom gas-rings had given me a mistaken notion of the word, I had looked it up in the dictionary and found that it alludes to hot springs.

Over the side of Carn Rynettin I tramped, and across the gully that divides it from the hill to the south.   As I topped the summit a hare suddenly rose from under my feet.   It fled with the sudden speed for which its heart is specially adjusted, giving me a fright for which my heart is not so obligingly arranged.

The Boiling Spring was on the downward slope of the hill, and was marked by a slanting stake and the incongruity of a china cup.   I craned over the edge of the tiny bank to cautiously insert a finger,

[1] *In the Shadow of Cairngorm*, Dr. Forsyth.

glad to remember that I had an application for burns in my pocket first-aid set.   It was a long way down in the hollow to the basin of water, and I nearly fell in with my efforts to reach it.   Trying to save myself from an unpremeditated hot bath, I plunged my whole hand into the bubbling well, and withdrew it very hastily.   For a moment I could not tell whether I was burnt or frozen, then I realised it was the intense cold that had stung !

Thinking that the heat might be below, but feeling that I was impiously meddling with the very centre of the Earth, I thrust my hand among the dancing grains of white sand that line the actual funnel, and the water suddenly spouted up to a height of four-teen inches, gushing gleefully into every crevice in my mackintosh that the rain had inadvertently missed.   I made my apologies, and when by its quietened action the spring seemed to be placated, I drank of it and went my way.   I have returned at other times of the year, but never to find it even at the heat which the boy described as " lukewarm because it looks warm and it isn't."   Even those who have lived near it all their lives have never felt the temperature to be anything other than the usual coolness of a spring, so it may be that the word Ghoile has been mistaken both in the Gaelic and English. Remote as the well is, it is a favourite trail for children on a Sunday.   They drink of it and watch its varying activity and return home unaware that they have been perpetuating the well worship of their ancestors, to whom clear water was a symbol of life.

Between the dark trees of Tor hill in Tulloch and

the darker Spey lies bonny Loch Garten, once the
haunt of the Glaistig or Banshee of the house of
Gartenmore.   Now family and ghost are both gone,
and the kelpie plays by himself where the water-
lilies float their lovely cups, sun and moon combined
in the silver petals and gold-tasselled centres.   I
have been assured more than once that at night
the blossoms all sink under water, to rise again in
the dawn from their dark hiding.   There is good
excuse for this mistake, for at nightfall the clos-
ing sepals are just the green-grey of the twilight,
and you may watch the flowers' brilliant whiteness
fade away and completely disappear while other
white objects stand more visible in the gathering
darkness.

Among the trees, smaller white flowers spring :
the Winter Evergreen like a primitive Lily of the
Valley, and the scarce Goodyera which looks as if it
had just been born and is just going to die.   Not
far away lies the Loch of the Curse, Loch Mallachie.
Nothing could look less accursed than this sparkling
water on a sunny day, with its two little pine-set
isles seemingly afloat on its vivacious surface.   If
this was the scene of a curse, the cause has been
forgotten, but there is evil on the stream that runs
out of the loch and down to the road at Mullin-
garroch.   There a bridegroom of Garten lost his
bride at the hour of the wedding.   She was young
and well, and yet, as she crossed the water, she
stepped a little uncertainly, stood still a moment
with a troubled look, and fell dead.

With all the pent-up force that anguish can
release, the man cried out that all newly married

couples passing in his steps should share his unhappy fate.

It is a nuisance on the marriage day to have to go
into the wood in order to cross the stream higher up ;
but whether you call such an act " nerves " or
" superstition," caused by " Fate " or " coincidence,"
later facts have undeniably added to the belief.

THE ROAD BY INSH

IN THE FOREST

In the Forest of Glenmore, in the dip of it that runs between the Luineag and the Druidh, in a sudden dell that often hides a herd of deer, I was wondering whether the staff in His Majesty's Stationery Office ever read the Forestry Reports and visualise this beauty. Do they go down through the white magic of space between the printed lines and come out—here?

Juniper, heather, and blaeberry hide the uneven ground and brush round the rough red trunk of ancient pine and weeping fir, decorating even the ant-hills with their bosky green. They run, not like a carpet, but like a choppy sea guiltless of foam, till the distance joins their tips to the tree tops.

Above me, but not high above me, for the trees here are more old than tall, the wind sighs. It goes here, and is lost; there, and is lost; till it seems strange that it is not visible in the form of ribboned mist binding the brotherhood of the pines. Overhead the foliaged weight moves laboriously, leisurely scenting the air with aromatic loveliness. As I was resting, a fir cone fell with a " plop " on to my head, and threw a brown seed into my open hand. To have the futility of one's existence accentuated in this manner is nothing short of insult. That fluttery little brown flange that lay on my palm will probably be enjoying the scene when I and my grandchildren and their children's children have all had our little day, for I carefully carried it to the open space of a new plantation and added " one " to the population of millions of green fir children.

Not that young firs are usually grown from seed on the spot; they are carefully reared in nurseries until about three years old. In former days the foresters marked at random such trees as they considered mature and trusted that enough fallen seeds would take root to replace the newly cut timber. It was not a far-seeing method. The remaining trees obscured the sun, the new generation was smothered by its elders, and the forests became poorly stocked.

In the early nineteenth century the Laird of Rothiemurchus and its woods started a new system; felling a section at a time, and railing off the bare place to protect the seedlings from the deer. The seedlings thus had light and air and thinned themselves automatically by the rule of Deil tak' the hindmaist.

It is strange to think that the forest floor only sees the open sunlight about once in every eighty or ninety years, and that some of the trees are direct descendants of the primeval forest in which man had no hand. The very word " forest " holds a thrill of anticipation. Did not all the stories of our young days really " begin " from the moment when the hero or heroine " came to a wood " ? The adventures of King Arthur's Knights, the magic of Merlin, were in the forest of Boceline, and the majority of the legends of Northern Europe have a background of forest scenery, woods full of strange beasts and beings, woods whose shadowed acres represented the mystery of night or the fearful regions that lie on the way to the land of the Dead.

In Britain the groves of the Druids were held sacred long after their religious cult had died out, and there are woods in Scotland where even in the nineteenth century it was considered unlucky to cut so much as a twig. The Calton Hill of Edinburgh, with the pillars of its unfinished memorial standing like petrified tree trunks, was at one time a sacred hazel grove, hence the name " Calltunn," a hazel.[1] On Speyside one may come across small plantations of oak that have been left unmolested because generations have handed down the tale of their sacred antiquity.

The people of many nations have trodden woodland tracks to make their sacrifices, their supplications, and to ease their sorrows at the altars of sylvan gods. It was a natural religious impulse to seek peace and aloofness among the dim-lit solitude of trees, and we still worship in the shadows of high avenues when we kneel in the nave of a Gothic Cathedral.

It would be surprising if the big forests of Inverness-shire were barren of rumour and tale, and indeed they are not. The King of the Faeries owns Glenmore, and in the early nineteenth century showed his interest in his people of Rothiemurchus by ridding them of inconvenient guests.

Before the crusie came into general use, the low-country tenantry of the Duke of Gordon were in the habit of making a yearly journey to Glenmore for

[1] *Forest Folklore*, Porteous.

the purpose of gathering fir-strips or gius.   These strips were gathered and stored, a small number being always kept ready to hand in the suacan or kindling-basket that hung beside the fire.   When ignited from the peat glow, these resinous splinters gave out a bright white light, equalling the illumination of five candles.   It was the duty of the man of the house to light the first gius with a word of gratitude for its fear-expelling comfort.

All the Duke of Gordon's people had the right to gather fir-candles in his forest of Glenmore, but the tenants from the south made themselves unpopular by quartering themselves and their horses on the far-from-wealthy population of Rothiemurchus.   The unwilling hosts could not refuse hospitality.   To take a man's cattle, or even to kill him, was manly and mannerly, but to refrain from offering food and shelter—nobody cared to take such guilt under their roof ; no, not though the meal bowie was empty and the scent of the kebbuck a mocking memory when the host gave " God-speed " to the departing guest.

It was not the Duke but the head of the Daoine Sith who finally took the matter in hand.

The visitors, busy with hatchet and knife, were suddenly faced by a supernatural figure of huge dimensions ; it came lashing through the trees whistling with rage and raising a hurricane in its path, a hurricane that twirled the pine-needles into spirals and shook the trees as with a storm.   The kindle-gatherers were fighters by necessity and by nature, but not of such a foe as this, and they quitted the scenes of their labour silently and swiftly and came no more to the domain of Domhnall Mor.

Out of the shadow of primeval forest mankind hewed his way to sunshine and prosperity; but still the trees gave heat, material for houses, for fences and utensils, and protection from the elements and wild beasts. Of more importance still, they verified most surely of all things in nature the return of spring and renewal of life after deathlike winter; so strengthening the sense of faith in a power greater than human. What wonder that trees were worshipped! The Maiden Tree of Glenmore, Maighdean Coire-chum-glaich, stood on the north side of Loch Morlich. The tree was felled in the early eighteenth century, and judging by the remaining plank, must have measured nineteen feet in girth. I have heard that the man who cut The Maiden was dismissed from the estate, which is suggestive of punishment for sacrilege; but whether the expulsion was actual or not, the fact remains that in the minds of present people such a decree seems not only a probability but a justifiable act. The Maiden was probably a descendant of a tree embodying a treespirit, which, though in advance of the earlier view of personification, is less advanced than the conception of an independent sylvan deity.

The Queen Tree of the forest that stood near the gate of the Dell was blown down as late as 1920, but still there remains the Faerie Tree with its thick trunk and massive outspreading branches to keep alive a memory of early beliefs and inspire a present sense of reverence.

Forests being so separate a manifestation of

nature, it is natural to expect that foresters would
have different characteristics from other men; but
on Speyside they cannot be singled out from the
gamekeepers and stalkers, who are all quiet people,
slow in movement, quick of eyesight, and full of
suppressed humour. In point of fact, very few men
work solely for the Forestry Commission, as the
active employment is periodical rather than constant,
so that the duties of stalker, gillie, gamekeeper,
guide, or agricultural hand is often combined with
that of tree-tending; and in some instances rabbit-
snaring is part of a forester's duty, from which the
Forestry Department makes a little addition to its
revenue. In fact, a forester's work has undergone
complete reversal since the days when Glenmore was
a royal forest. The trees then grew without
hindrance or aid, more of them than man knew how
to use, and the condition of the timber did not
matter so long as it sheltered and did not interfere
with the game; whereas now if a hind wishes to
make a meal of a young fir, it is not the fir that is
allowed to suffer.

It was to the preservation of the deer that Robert
Stewart was to give his attention when he was
sheltered under the term " Forester of Glenmore "
from the punishment due a deserter from Argyll's
forces. Stewart in his position of Subaltern had
refused to take part in the massacre of Glencoe as
soon as he fully understood the brutal orders, but
the trees of Glenmore and its owner, the Duke of
Gordon, hid him successfully from the avenging
hand.

The Foresters may well claim to be an Ancient

Order if they include the Inspector of Woods of the
Royal Domain of Pharaoh Teto, who is mentioned
in a document dated some 3500 years before Christ.[1]

When tramping here, there, where the path led,
as the wind blew, I was often asked whether I was
not afraid to be alone in the forests. On enquiry
as to what I needed to fear, the reply was always,
" Nothing but the loneliness," and one or two
added, " and the eeriness," and the remark was
often followed by tales of strange lights or in-
explicable sounds.

I have seen no phenomena and heard no faerie
music, but I *have* been afraid in the forest. I have
been afraid at twilight; feeling helplessly small
among the tall and powerful population of trees as
daylight deserted the winding paths, and the cool
hush that is evening spread among the innumerable
columns. I have been afraid of the silence when the
birds ceased their song, leaving spaces in the bushy
foliage that had been filled with melody. Small
pools take on an impossible depth in the half-light,
and the rising moon brings with it a thousand
shadow-trees, black half-brothers, to lie aslant the
actual stalwart trunks. I have been troubled at a
lost breeze that stirred the tops with a sigh, and have
been startled to immovability when a deer leapt
suddenly across the path, nothing showing but a
flying shadow and a streaking flange of white—the
miracle of its silent disappearance more awful than
its unexpected arrival. Yes, I have been afraid in
the forest, but there are various qualities of fear, and
forest-fear has a depth difficult to explain, a secret

[1] *Forest Folklore*, Porteous.

appeal to the subconsciousness that allies it more with beauty than alarm.

It was in an alder copse that I learnt the secret of Harry Lauder's cromag. I had asked a forester to cut me a walking-staff, and was told that I would need to wait a week as it was " no use cutting it against the moon." Timber cut when the moon is fulling will lie green and twist, but if cut when the moon is on the wane it will dry soon and lie straight. This statement of fact sounded at first like deference to Diana, but it seemed unlikely that a modern Forestry Department should consider her or work by superstition. If the moon can pull the tides of the sea, is it so incredible that it should have some effect upon the miles of sleeping trees and their rising sap? Over a thousand years ago Pliny gave the advice, " never to touch timber except when the moon is on the change," and that " the pine should be rooted up when the moon is on the wane "; and though his additional conditions " that the South wind should be blowing and operations not begun till after mid-day " suggest a short working week, he was evidently right in the main fact, as is frequently proven in the forests to-day.

Various people in the district have assured me that a pig should be killed at the fulling of the moon as it then weighs more, and I have certainly seen a very groggy penful of chicks that were hatched against the moon alongside a healthy batch that had apparently been consulting the calendar.

The moon may " have a face like the clock in the hall " when seen from other places, but on Speyside the shadows show an old man who cut firewood from a sacred grove and was thrown into the moon for punishment, where you may see him carrying his faggots and never arriving home till the moon shall die.

The wealth that lay in timber was not realised until the York Building Co. exploited it in 1728. Up to that time the tenants had been in the habit of paying the Laird 1s. 8d. for the amount that a man could cut in a year. The requirements were small, being only as much as was needed for domestic fuel or sufficient to make charcoal for the work of the smithies.

The present Forestry Department owns over thirty-nine thousand acres of land, which includes fifty Scottish forests—even the covered slopes of Speyside alone look like a goodly supply of wood; but timber takes long to mature, and there is really surprisingly little material in each tree when it comes under the saw, so that we are obliged to import window-frames, cabinet-ware, doors, tool-handles, boxes, and furniture to the tune of £10,000 a year, and an even more surprising figure to be added is £49,000 worth of raw timber, part of which consists of pit props. Sweden is draining its bogs to make way for forests, yet miles of timber-growing land lies barren in Scotland.

One would expect in these forest homes that every boy would be brought up with a pocket-knife and a piece of wood in his hands; that cradles and cupboards, kists and stools would be the individual work of various families; and that the long winter evenings would be spent turning odd lumps of wood into attractive articles for sale to summer

visitors, as in the Tyrol and the Black Forest.   But
quite to the contrary ; even the carving class at Aviemore did not get sufficient support to continue.
There is a twofold reason for this lack of craftsman-
ship.

There is hardly an individual between Kingussie
and Ballindalloch that is not related to the Lairds of
Grant or MacKintosh or Shaw or MacDonald ; the
veriest crofter's laddie has high blood in his veins,
and if he shows it in courtly speech and irreproach-
able manners, he also shows it by standing with his
hands in his pockets looking over the landscape
when any other boy would be actively employed.
As he grows up, he dances and makes love as his
fathers did before him, but he does not make a foot-
ball pitch of every piece of green ground, and he
will not be cajoled into labour after his working
hours.

The second reason I found out for myself, by
offering to chop some firewood.   I expected a good
axe with a three-foot haft to be a thing of destructive
joy, and I hurled its gleaming edge at the first half-
rotted log in masterly anticipation.   The log
bounced away—and though under more persistent
application the axe bit in, it then required a wrestling
match to dislodge the weapon.   It is not at all
surprising that the people do not carve the forest
wood.   Nothing but a machine-driven saw can
make any impression on its close-grained durability.

CASTLE GRANT

(page 179)

THE GRANTS' TOWN

It is over five hundred years since the noble de Grant came in on the French tide from the South, and roved from Stratherrick to Cromdale and gradually got and begot until all was Grant property from northern to southern Craigellachie where the Clan cried " Stand sure," and later " Stand fast," and stood both sure and fast to the lands it had acquired while continuing to add by purchase and marriage till Glen Urquhart and Cullen joined Abernethy.

Congash was probably the first of the Strathspey holdings, and it is still a place of interest though there is nothing left now of the old manor house.

A small glen runs down to the Cromdale road, one bank supporting the big farm with its imposing steading while the other shelters a most unbelievable cottage standing among a tangle of raffia-bright weeds, its door guarded by the down-curved branch of a tree, and the " made by hand " appearance enhanced by the broken line of the crevassed stones, as if Nature had been busy with a fine pen and black ink.

In a field behind the farm, the brown of the loam is interrupted by a large circle filled with tumbled stones overgrown with grass and bramble ; a patch of undisciplined vegetation in the midst of orderly cultivation. Yet, when the Chapel stood beside the circle, it was a sanctuary of culture in a wilderness. The ancient graveyard now grows good oats, but many of the standing stones remain, among them two that are incised with the elephant-dolphin and with the fan, with whorls and the floral-tipped zigzag that has been lately cited as the possible origin of the Fleur-de-lis ; " liss " being given as old Gaelic for " lios," indicating a " garden," and the sign denoting the herbal skill of the Druids.[1]

Cromdale, lying two miles farther up the road, belonged to the Earls of Fife and of Menteith and to the family of Nairn before the Grants took it over in 1609. It no longer has the appearance of a burgh town ; one would not guess that it had had its Courthouse, its Jail, and its Fair. It was the latter that brought the town's downfall, for at the Fair two factions of the Grants had a quarrel, and in those days opinions were rammed home and the bodies buried after. One half of the attackers withdrew from the burgh town as a result of the fight and set up house at the gates of Castle Grant, and that was the end of Cromdale's prosperity and importance.

The battle which later famed its Haughs to song was more noted for its element of surprise than for any influence it had upon the history of the time. General Buchan had been sent over from Ireland by King James to take up arms on his behalf. As the General lay asleep with his followers at a spot near Dalchapple, General MacKay made an early morning descent and interrupted the Jacobites' dreams, driving them broadcast, without even giving them time to dress. It was not a battle but a rout, and

[1] Hon. Erskine of Marr, in a newspaper article.

would have been a wholesale slaughter if the mountain mist, the friend of the Stewarts, had not enfolded the helpless Jacobites.

Castle Grant cannot be seen from the road, for elm and larch grow alongside the sweeping drives almost up to the door, hiding the tall tower with its low flanking wings and showing only the broken surface of slate gables and snowy flagstaff. It is a puzzling edifice. It faces back to front, has four different names, and consists of more than one style of architecture. An MS. of 1489 refers to " The messuage " of Freuchie, which was probably a manor house standing on the hillock which lies a quarter of a mile to the south-east of the present Castle.

One of the early tales connected with the building as Castle Freuchie introduces Ian Craoithe or Hard Ian, who plotted successfully with the MacGregors for the taking of the Castle. His daughter married a MacGregor, perhaps she was the reason and the reward of his assistance. The Castle had belonged to the Comyns, and the skull of the captured owner lies in the Castle to this day. It is kept in a cupboard, an awesome sight, cut in half and hinged to hold, between brain and jaw, documents referring to Grant possessions. Grim humour : but the Comyn has ceased to chew the cud of forced thought, for the lower jaw has been lost, and if the yellow cranium be lost also, the property will no longer belong to a Grant.

Another name for the home of the Grants was Ballachasteil, the Castle of the Pass perhaps, or the Town Castle, and under this name is told the tale of a young Laird of Grant who, being under age, was brought up by his grandfather at Ballindalloch while his uncle enjoyed all the privileges of life at Ballachasteil.   Apparently nobody but the uncle himself enjoyed his tenure, for when the boy was of age and happened to go into the Castle for a rest while out hunting, the inmates, the tenants, and servants all claimed him as Laird and threw the uncle out with small ceremony.

The next name also has a story attached, and something a little more substantial to warrant it, for it concerns Babbette, and the centre and oldest part of the Castle is known as Babbette's Tower.   Part of the tower dates from the fifteenth century ; and, as you tread the stone stair carpeted with ancient Grant tartan, and see the six-foot thickness of the walls that curve for no obvious reason, suggestive of hidden passages and secret ways, you are conscious of the height and the strength of this battlemented keep and the sincerity and craft of its workmanship.

Down a curling passage—turn to the right—and deep-set in the gloom of the wall is a door.   It looks as if it would only lead to a press, but the words shine out, " The Tapestry Room."   This is also Babbette's Room, this is the Haunted Room.   All round the walls the tapestry runs, a magic landscape of greeny-blue or bluey-green, throwing an eerie light about the room as if the sun shone through blue foliaged trees.   One would think that the hidden door, once discovered, might lead into the woven wood, but it only gapes into a blackness ; a blackness into which, according to tradition, Babbette the

Fair was thrust until she would obey her father's wishes.

This may be the inner history of the mystery of the marriage contract of Barbara Grant, daughter of John the Gentle. The name must surely have been given in irony, for the man's deeds were far from effeminate—John the Gentle was out with Huntly more than once " creating terror " !

On July 26th, 1568, a contract of marriage was made between Barbara Grant and Robert Munro the younger of Fowlis.[1] From the Laird's point of view it was not much of a match, and apparently some one else was displeased also, for the day after the contract was signed, one, Colin MacKenzie of Kintail, gave bond of manrent to the Grant vowing to defend him against the Clan Ranald. Would that not be the reason that in 1570, the previous arrangement not having materialised, a new contract was made by Gentle John for his daughter Barbara to wed Colin of Kintail? The first match may have been a case of near hearts but far properties. Judging by her mother's marriage and death, Barbara would be about eighteen at the time, and may have had her own ideas about adhering to the original arrangement. If she had, they were overcome, for two years later the contract with Colin was ratified, and more and more promises were extracted from him for the defence of Grant under increasingly binding oaths, until no un-named enemy was left in all the land !

The Barbara of the story died in the dark rather than yield, which was the correct procedure for a

[1] *The Chiefs of Grant,* Sir Wm. Fraser.

heroine in such circumstances, but when the cupboard was discovered and opened some fifty years ago it revealed, not a young girl's skeleton, but— muskets ! The men who stacked the muskets in the racks which are still to be seen below the shelves that store the household linen may have trampled Babbette's bones to dust, but in any case they would be more anxious than ever to keep the haunting story alive, so that any sounds which might be overheard would be added to the previous tale. From the position and the deep curving wall, it would seem likely that a passage with a descending stair led from the inside of the improvised armoury.

A deeper mystery of the Haunted Room of Castle Freuchie concerns the weaving of the tapestry ; ¡for tradition holds that it was worked by " Twenty-two ladies in exile."   Who they were and why they were exiled nobody knows, but a synonym for exile which is common to all parts of Scotland is the expression " Gang t' Freuchie," signifying " Taking to the heather," the place-name coming from the old dative " Fraochaigh " in the Gaelic.[1]   So it may be, that while sympathetic visitors look mournfully at the work, imagining the threads interwoven with nostalgia, the twenty-two ladies chuckle in their sleeves at the simplicity of a joke that has lasted so long !

On the way down the stair, the picture of an old henwife looks both " at " and " past " you, for she is gley-eyed, and resembles some wicked old character out of an ancient and horribly truthful ballad. Half a witch I would say, and bad company for the

[1] Professor Watson of Edinburgh University.

hens, but she is said to have run her part of the
estate with good profit for the Laird.

Down below is the dining-room; a most important part of the Castle if it is true that " Cha bhi
gean air Granndaich gus am faigh iad lite," " the
Grants are never gracious till they get their porridge."

AN OLD-FASHIONED CORNER IN GRANTOWN

The long walls are of stone with inset arches, but
they are covered with panelling of wood, and that
is almost covered with pictures, portraits of those
who have sat at the head of the table of Grant.

What a variety of talents the family exhibited!
Going farther back than the portraits and farther
afield than the direct heirs, there were caterans and
plunderers like Sheumas an Tuim or Sheumas na
Creach, who, with the help of his cousin Huntly,
slew most of the men of Deeside in revenge for
the murder of his brother-in-law. Huntly had
adopted the orphans of this raid, and their number

being many, they fed from a trough and were seen thus at their meal by Sheumas when he was on a later visit. This thirteenth Laird of Grant was rather overcome both by the result of his revenge and the kind-heartedness of his cousin, so he gathered the children from one side of the trough and took them to Speyside to be Grants, while the others remained and became Gordons.

There was a Grant who excelled at wood-carving, and many who excelled at carving their foes. A Grant of Tulloch was known as " Donull na h'iteag," Donald the Feather, for his dancing, and another remains in my memory because he was heavily fined for not having made his wife go to Church for two years. She had a priest in the house, but that did not help as an excuse, indeed it only made matters worse, for the priest was not licensed. The Laird protested that in the first place he was not responsible for his wife, a statement which would hardly be accepted without a smile in 1685. He added that the Parish Church had been vacant for a year, and further, that the next nearest one was six miles away, and above all that his wife had been ill, but all this logic availed him nothing, and the Church collection was the richer for 42,500 pounds Scots !

The Champion Boatman, Alasdair Mor, was only eighteen when he set out for London with his boat on his back. The curragh was easily portable and must have been an object of interest to the Londoners who had slighted the Spey and its watermen in favour of the Thames. If they were surprised at the craft, they were even more surprised at the boat-man, who justified his Laird's boast that no one could

OLD SPEY BRIDGE

(page 189)

outstrip him.   No boat on the river could get near
the little circular barque that skimmed about like
a leaf before a storm, with Alasdair Grant's long
legs curled miraculously into its limited cavity.
The admiring populace filled the lad's bonnet with
golden pieces, and had their final surprise when he
handed his entire gains to his Master with the
request that the Laird would present it to the Lady
of Grant that she might buy pins.   The boatman
is honoured with a full-sized portrait in the Hall at
Castle Grant, and beside his picture is a painting of
" The Piper."   If the one could row the other
could blow, and he took on a wager that he would
pipe all the way from Inverness and three times
round the Castle without a pause.   It can be seen
by the architecture in the picture that the Castle had
no abutting wings at that time, but it must have
seemed at least two miles in circumference to the
Piper by the time he had raised the tune without
ceasing for a distance of over twenty-five miles.
Round he went for the first time, with his heart
pounding as if to break his body and sounding to
him like a big drum above the roar of his pipes.
Round again with nothing but red to be seen
through the bloodshot curtain of his eyes.   Once
more round, with staggering feet and breath that
sobbed to the bag, and back to the completed circuit,
where, amid shouts and cries of distress, the Piper
filled her again and marched off over the unmapped
moors of Eternity to give a piobaireachd to the long-
lost Lairds of Grant.

Beside the pictures and up the stair it is musket
and lance, musket and lance all the way, and the

arms are overhung by ancient flags, some of them
so reduced as to be only the merest remnants, as if
their grey net enmeshed the abstract of Time and
cared nothing for the scrap of discoloured silk that
betokened the regimental incident.   In the main
Hall also, sword, targe, and drum decorate every
inch of the wall, and the ceiling is fiercely starred
with the spears of the Fencibles.

The Grant Fencibles were raised in 1793, and
Frazer and Glengarry and Lochaber followed suit.
Jacobite feeling died down very quickly on Speyside,
but the Grants in any case were not quite sure how
much of such feeling they had at the time of the '45.
They chased a few prisoners after Culloden and then
became definitely Government men, though they
were poorly requited for the loyalty they gave.

The main approach of Castle Grant from the
north brings you to a studded door set flush in a
wall of a hundred windows ; and no wonder that
Queen Victoria, on arriving at it, compared the
Castle to a factory.   The older frontage from the
south shows the pile of Babbette's Tower, tall,
thick-walled, and loopholed, with balconied battle-
ments and crow-stepped gable.   From it, two low-
set wings stretch south to form a raised courtyard
reached by a flight of steps.   It is a perfect castle
entrance ; an iron gate, a swinging bell to clang, and
the deep baying of dogs to greet the sound of footsteps on the large flagstones.   A dairymaid may
trip across with a bowl of cream in her hands and a
kitten at her heels, for the dairy is on one side and
offices adjoining the kitchen on the other, and
beneath them is the old brew-house and the place

where the candle-dips were made.   Up at the North
Lodge, a stair leads to the private railway station
which is on the property, and that is why the railway
bridge across the public road is in such good taste
as to match the architecture of the Castle's gate.

The tale of the Grants of Freuchie is the history
of Inverness-shire in miniature ; a progression from
inter-warfare of the Clans to the combination of
forces which were later split by the claims of two
religions and two kings.   Cattle, crops, sheep, and
forestry have kept the successive Lairds to the front
as model landowners.   " An improver in this way
is one of the greatest patriots of the kingdom," wrote
Sir Ludovic in 1760, and he added the information
that after assisting his tenants with money and gear
he found that he was increasing his rent roll by £300
a year.

No town has more right to its name than Grantown, founded as it was by the Good Sir James in
1766 as a result of the quarrel at Cromdale which
settled a little Grant community at his Castle gate.
Am Bhaile Ur, the " New Town " as it was first
called, was simply planned in the days when such
items as drains and gas-works presented no difficulty,
and it still keeps the appearance of a favourite child
carefully set upon the heather and told to keep its
pinafore clean.

There are many quaint little cottages at the foot
of the village cuddling their backs into the hill, but
the oldest part is nearer the Castle, mocked by the
hideous boxes of the new housing scheme.   It is
not easy, when treading the trim grass plots that
line the square, or resting under the shade of the

old trees framing the road, to visualise the horrible scenes of censure and cruelty that took place when the Old Regality Cross was the centre ornament. Although it raised a grey head above the gaping crowds, its feet were stained red with human blood. The heart of the judge must have been harder than the stone, when he condemned Margaret Bain to a scourging, to the loss of an ear, and to banishment for " haunting with the Halkit Steir and Glendry Broken men and Keithren." She came from the folded peace of Inchtomie, from the heather homes of the caterans, to dark imprisonment in Castle Grant, to public punishment, to exile. With the very sound of such a name comes a vision of a fair-haired girl, unjustly treated for kindly acts to hunted men ; but in fairness it must be noted that there is mention of " other faults " in the record of con-demnation, and Margaret may have been a thor-oughly wicked character with years of ugly tales written on her face. At any rate, the Halkit Steir and his band made no attempt at rescue, though the hero of the cattle-raiders could not be accused of cowardice. His name, Gamhainn Cirinn in the Gaelic, implied that he had a white mark on his face, and he is never mentioned by his real name, though it is presumed that he came of Lochaber stock. The Chief of Grant, having been ordered by the Com-mittee of Estates to apprehend the raider, first com-plained that his tenants refused to give assistance, and then, having successfully roped the Steir, seemed to regret the success of the capture, and despatched an urgent message with the bodyguard to Edin-burgh urging that the Halkit Steir should be

released on " good securitie," and requesting that
meantime protection should be given to the Grant
property against the wrath of the MacDonalds, who
were presumably related.   So Gamhainn was seen
again in the shadows of Glenmore, protected and,
during his last illness, nursed, by the recalcitrant
crofters.

At the foot of the village of Grantown, beyond the
pine woods, the Spey runs swiftly under Wade's
Bridge ; a massive structure, with intimate beauty
in its uneven span, with pride of strength in its great
buttresses crowned by inset parapet.   It still looks
absolutely reliable in spite of the iron stitches, over
a hundred of them, that bind its stones against the
swirling press of the dark water.   It withstood the
attack of the Spey in the '29 flood, though the
hurricane deprived one span of its surface, all but
the parapet having crumbled into the river.   On to
this perilous pathway hanging above the roaring
waters a man stepped out.   He fought his way
across, swaying as an occasional blast swept down
the river, so that those on the bank hid their faces
rather than witness a tragedy which they were
powerless to prevent.   The man had been given a
message to take to a farmer's wife on the other side
—and he took it.

Fired by the example, a pedlar hoisted his wares
on to his back after the manner of a pack pony, and
amid encouragement and hysterical laughter successfully negotiated the same narrow track.   Now word
has gone forth that the river is winning the fight,
that the bridge is doomed, but even when the new
bridge is in use, there is surely no need to destroy

the old.   Let it be left for the sole use of the wraith
of Lord Charles Hay who was responsible for the
regiment who built it in 1754, and of the proud
mason who added his mark after the word " Ended "
on the inscription.

In summer time on the river, between this bridge

STONE OF OLD SPEY BRIDGE

and Inverallan, children in gay paddling suits make
use of little sandy bays to play at " seashore " ;
building sand-castles and decorating them with
tansy and scabious, with cinquefoil and wild roses
that grow within hand's reach.   The small chintz
dresses and gaudy buckets stand out against the
background of sullen sepia waters, as butterflies
would flutter on the black edge of the Pit.

The path winds near the Figgat Well and one-time market-place of the Fair that was transferred from Kincardine to the site of the old Church of Inverallan, where the river is encroaching on the thickly populated graveyard, sweeping its walls with curving waters and rushing with a hissing sound past the stone cauldron and incised stone that guards a moaning gate.

Inverallan was an early possession of the Grants, and in its old mansion, long since destroyed, Prince Charlie slept the night before Culloden. The key now hangs in the Hall at Castle Grant; an eight-inch mockery of rusty iron which would need to turn in empty air to unlock a phantom house which no one but the angry old river remembers.

TOWARDS THE SOUTH

Rain and rain and rain. Solid loads of water hit my mackintosh and splattered from its hard surface in a mist that was only interrupted by the steady stream that ran from the brim of my hat. Each step brought a sucking sound as miniature tides rose and fell in my shoes. The cottages at Druimguish were seen as if through tears, and the witch's pot swinging from the branch of the tree which marks the eight-mile track to Feshie Lodge seemed aboil from the spray which the drops raised in the level of its full supply. I was vowing to myself to take in future the advice given me by an old Highlander and replace my mackintosh with a plaid. " It 's not rain, but the wind combined with the rain that harms you," he had told me, " and once a plaid is well soaked it is windproof and keeps you warm through the worst the weather can do."

There was no need to worry this time, however, for the downpour was too torrential to last, and it cleared as I topped the long stretch of moor. The sudden black anger of the clouds turned to sullen grey mists that retreated up the sides of Meall Bhuidhe and Creag Dhubh, leaving the trees beyond Carstilbeag vivid and ashine ; just in the manner that the leaves of the coltsfoot may be fingered from cobweb grey to varnished brightness. Rounding the shoulder of Creag na Sroine, I could hear the

FESHIE BRIDGE

(page 193)

vivacious Feshie repeating its own name as a continuous splash before I caught sight of its boulder-
strewn course. Across the water the house of the
Tod-hunter looked uninhabited except for a mist
of blue above the chimney, and I passed along by
the little school-house where five small coats hung
on the pegs and five small heads worried (perhaps
not overmuch) as to "how soon a train travelling
at fifty miles an hour would," etc., while the
wind played with the larch twigs, and the freshing
of the river was louder than the teacher's voice,
and the reflected light from the snow patch below
Badden Mosach cast a white illumination on
the class-room wall. This snow is the perpetual
shroud of a girl named Margaret who died here
after wandering distracted in the hills. She had
lost her reason because the MacKintosh had jilted
her, and she cast the curse of the man of Clury on
the family.

The little bridge that is slung over the river like
a spider's web makes it possible to get across to the
ancient burial-ground. If, as tradition has it, the
last person to be buried has the duty of keeping
guard over the other graves, some one here has had
a long watching that is not likely to end until the
roar of the Last Day shall swallow up the glen.
The restless peace of this river-haunted corrie is
sufficient companionship, and the voice of man has
a foreign sound in such a place; yet here, at the foot
of the crag-crowned Coire Garbhlach, the great
cattle tryst was held, the market which preceded the
Falkirk Fair. Through the thick pine woods the
footpath runs to a building which might be described

as a hut enclosing a hut, though nothing but the
chimney-stalk of the original inner bothy remains.
No other part of the building matters, however, for
on the plaster above the first fireplace is the picture
by Landseer of two stags and a hind. The artist
was a guest of the Duchess of Bedford when she
rented Glen Feshie Lodge, and here and there in
Badenoch one comes across Landseer's portrait set
in high esteem near a photo of the Minister or an
engraving of some much-loved Laird. Sometimes a
more valuable memorial falls from the pages of an
old-fashioned book ; a pencil portrait of the present
owner's mother or aunt, or of some favourite dog
now well away over the borders of Time.

The river beside the Lodge is undetermined, and
chooses now this channel, now that, among the stone-
heaped islands ; and the tall spires of the Meuran
nan Sith or Faerie Fingers bow to the unseen Good-
folk as they pass.

This glen has a traditional reputation of being
thickly populated with the Daoine Sith. Certainly
I have seen a group of foxgloves gracefully bending
when no breath of wind stirred the air, and on
reaching them have found that they no longer moved,
though other plants at a distance had by then taken
up the movement. The first faerie tale of the glen
that I heard was of a man some sixty years ago who
had his plaid wrenched from him on a night of
perfect calm. " Very well, then, you may have it,"
he said to the unseen assailants, and continued on
his way. On returning next day, his plaid came
sailing through the air before him and spread over
a rock by the path. Another tale was of a man who

refused to step aside or remove his bonnet when the Daoine Sith passed him ; a custom which even townsfolk have not lost.   So it was removed for him and he was thrown his length on the ground, though there was no storm to account for the episode. Because these stories show a similar local theme, I looked to the meteorologists and found that Glen Feshie is peculiarly subject to summer whirlwinds that travel the length of the glen and would easily account for every item of the tales ; a point which shows truthfulness of narration and the necessity to hand on information exactly as it is given.   Here, the oldest trees in Badenoch cling to the sloping ground with roots outspreading the width of their branches ; and seen from the shadow of the precipice of The Old Woman on the one hand, and Creag na Gaibhre on the other, the sudden slope of Sron na Ban-righ catches the higher lights.   This hill was the temporary throne of Mary Queen of Scots from which she watched the burning of the forests. Perhaps she did not intend to utterly destroy the wood which she considered held too important a place in her husband's estimation, but a good-going forest fire takes more than the word of a Queen to extinguish it.

If Queen Mary found the Scottish climate cold after the sunshine of France, she certainly made large enough fires to warm her hands, for even if the destruction of Badenoch Forest is not guaranteed by history, the same cannot be said of the burning of the Earl of Huntly's forests.

According to a tale, there was an incendiary on the spot long before the days of the Stewart Queen.

The King of Lochlann was envious of the Scottish forests and made novel use of his foster-mother in persuading her to undertake a journey of destruction. This Muime rained fire on all the Northern forests till she reached Badenoch, and there she met an unexpected death through the ruse of a Badenoch man.   He separated the kids from the goats, the lambs from their dams, the calves from the cows, thereby creating such a din of bellowing and bleating that the Dubh-Ghiubhais, as she is sometimes called, peeped out from the security of the clouds, and the man took the opportunity to shoot her with a silver sixpence.   By the last token, the dame has walked down the ages to the years of witch cult, but at any rate she has left some wonderful old pines in Glen Feshie, some of them surviving at a height of 1750 feet above sea-level.

General Wade had the notion to include this route to Deeside in his list of highways, Queen Victoria expressed the desire that it should be made a regular road, and now the Ministry of Transport is considering the possibility of its construction.

I expect the new road would cross the moor by Druimguish to Kingussie, but a lovely track runs into Kincraig under the frowning screes of Creag Mhigeachaidh, where occasional avalanches come down with ominous roars which may be enjoyed since the road is well clear of the danger.   It was on this route, before it drops to the lower ground, that I disturbed some snipe and happened to mention it to a shepherd.   " There is always thunder about when the snipe behave like that," he announced, and quoted an ancient Beltane song which he thought he had remembered from an old book [1]; anyhow, he said it was " in his head somewhere."   The translation runs, " Here 's to every little bird of the air save the snipe, but may she break her one foot going in at the door of her master ! "   Why such animosity against the snipe he was unable to say.   The Gaelic name agrees with the Irish and the French in calling the bird " Goat-of-the-Air " or " Sky-bleater," from the sound it makes when disturbed ; but the Lettish and the old German name is " Thunder-goat," and the early Scandinavian term was " The Thorsday Horse."   So the snipe is a Thunder Bird ; a reputation probably earned from the drumming sound of its wings (a sound which in volume is out of all proportion to the size of the bird), and from its habit of restlessness before bad weather.   Therefore this handmaid of Thor is not to be fed at Beltane, lest storms result ; instead, she is to be discouraged by being maimed like her Master the Thunder-god.

We spoke that day of all birds in the district ; from the Lord Eagle and the Capercaillie to the Little Clans of the Bushes, for we both knew the restless Redstarts of Abernethy, the Dippers and the Sand-pipers, the red-stockinged Oyster-catchers and the Crested and more ordinary Tits.   It was one of the last that gave me a few moments which still remain as an island of beauty in the sea of daily trivialities.

I was resting in the forest when a blue-bonnet arrived with a flurring of wings and actually settled on my elbow !   He adjusted his feathers, blue, black, and primrose-gold, and then poured out a spray of

[1] Probably Dr. Forsyth's *In the Shadow of Cairngorm.*

melody.   Quivering notes, like the sound of tiny
glass bells echoing across the water, clear and
decisive, phrased and replete with expression, they
spread miraculously among the tall columns of the
dim forest.   All that Nature holds of purity and
beauty had escaped suddenly from a ball of blue
feathers.

A twist of the decorative head, an enquiring
glance from a piercing black eye, a thrummel of
wings, a draught on my cheek, and the little songster
was gone; leaving a silence that hurt as a definite
pain, and an agony of dumbness, quickened by the
distant answer of another bird.

It was on the way to Glen Feshie that I heard the
Curlew crying as if one bird alone traversed the
whole length of the glen to be lost in the terrifying
wastes of Gaik.   " Gaik of the dark, wind-whistling,
crooked glens "; Gaik with its raven-river the Bran;
Gaik of the curse which says, " Diol Bhaltair an
Gaig ort," wishing you the fate of Walter Comyn;
for at the " Fenian Men's Leap," where Bran
Cottage now stands, beside the meeting of the waters,
the Comyn was torn to death by eagles, and the
women of Ruthven had good reasons to bless the
Bird of the Sun for their intervention, for the Lord
Walter was on his way to carry out his project of
forcing them to work in the fields unclothed.

A more recent and veritable incident of Gaik
which still finds a place among the tellers of tales in
Kingussie is of the bad Captain MacPherson who
went hunting with some companions in December
of the year 1800.   As the short hours of light did
not permit of return the same day, the party passed

the night in a bothy which was " the only human habitation for 30 square miles."   Late in the night, strange noises were heard as of some large creature scrambling about on the roof, accompanied by thunderous bangs and a " swishing sound such as a fishing-rod would make if used as a whip."   The men were terrified to silence, the dogs cowered in the corner with bristling hair, and added to the general discomfort by their low whines of fear.   At last the Captain rose and went out.   He was heard speaking in the darkness, and the answers he received were voiced in goat-like tones upbraiding him for bringing so few men.   The party returned the next day, and when the Captain set out on the morning of December 31st, only one of the previous companions would consent to go again ; a man Mac-Farlan, who was noted for his piety.   Once more the night was spent in the bothy, but the first eerie sound was the roar of a snow avalanche which completely covered and destroyed the hut.   A certain amount of apprehension had been felt at Kingussie because the Captain had left his watch and keys at home, an unprecedented occurrence, and a search party was soon on the track.   MacFarlan's body could not be found until a man who had previously found a corpse in the snow joined the search.   He justified this tradition (which is probably no more than the added experience of knowing what to look for), and discovered the remains of MacFarlan a long way from the bothy.

At the mouth of the glen, Tromie Bridge straddles sturdily across the brawling river, and the road runs round by Insh, passing the Lochs of

Dread and Balnespick—" the Bishops' place "—
which is set in seemly position above the Manse.
The road, guarded by a strange wall whose thin
stone slabs in lieu of posts hold the running wire,
slopes down to the blue beauty of Loch Insh where
Kincraig lies topsy-turvy in the shallow waters;
where boats are on land and trees and sky are in the
water, and the Spey swirls urgently to its meeting
with the Feshie.

FIDDLES AND FIRELIGHT

I WAS surprised one day on coming to the edge of a wood, to hear the strains of a violin. A sawmill stood at the side of a clearing, and across the unstable hills of sawdust I saw the musician facing the wooden wall of the shed to which his music was fastened. It was midday, and the other men sat eating, feet contentedly accentuating the rhythm; apparently as accustomed to concerts at mealtime as the clientele of a city restaurant. They had not seen me, and I crept away, afraid that my presence might spoil the unconscious atmosphere. Music for its own sake, played and accepted without the least self-consciousness, surrounded by the medium from which the instrument was made, in the wood-world where lilt had birth, seemed a very satisfying impression to hoard in the memory.

Nearly every cottage on Speyside has its singer, its piper, or fiddler, who plays for his own or his family's joy. I have heard skilful playing, tunes of dance, of opera, and those precious fragments handed down from one musician to the next, but nothing has ever erased the tune that was played on the edge of the wood.

The bagpipes are heard " on occasions." A meeting, a marriage, a celebration of any sort brings out the " breath of Scotland," but the fiddlers are like the crickets that chirrup contentedly on the hearthstone. There is no talk of style, no seeking of teachers; and that so large a percentage of the scattered population should play so difficult an instrument without any instruction other than occasional advice from relation or friend, is most surprising. The owner of a Jacobus Stainer dated 1690, a superb player himself, admitted that it was a good idea to allow a musical child to be " guided " by a good violinist, as the beginner was thus saved from getting into bad habits. Regular lessons twice a week and superintended practice were not suggested. He advised youth to learn and practise the old tunes till they were part of the player. " The original pure Scottish airs must be the foundation," he said, " from which all the pupil's music is to be built. Let him play the best of every country, the most difficult, but always hear within himself the simple melodies of his own land."

The description of a violin lesson in the West would not be recognised on Speyside, where fiddle and instruction are both readily handed round, always with the hope of finding or assisting in the making of another Neil Gow.

" Which finger shall I raise? " asks the Western pupil.

" Hast thou tobacco? " is the teacher's reply.

" Which finger shall I lift? "

" Hast thou tobacco? "

" No."

" Then lift and lay them down as it may please thyself."

Tradition gives every Clan and also every parish its own bard, and many a nameplace tells of the esteem in which singer and piper was held, such as Bhardaidh in Abernethy. Tulloch was famed for more than its Reel, of which the Browns of Kincardine are the first recorded players. Its native hero, John Roy Stewart, composed reels, marches, and psalm tunes, and from there came " Cairngorm " and " The Bonny Wife of Revack." The Reel of Tulloch with the stamp of victory in its intoxicating virility gives here and there a hint of the tragedy that followed the first glad sound of it.

A Grant known as Fear Thulach, head of the petty Chieftains of that Clan, held the lands of Tulloch in wadset, and had for a family one son, Allan, and a daughter, Iseabel Dubh Thulach. The Howdie who was tending the infant girl was overheard mumbling that the child, if she lived, would bring bloodshed and mischief on the Clan. However, the daughter did not share the fate of Deirdre's childhood, and the result of her freedom was an attachment at an early age to Ian Dubh Gear MacGrigor.

Her choice was unfortunate. Both families refused to countenance the marriage. Dark Iseabel and her lover were determined not to be easily parted, though their infrequent meetings were invariably interrupted. On returning from one of these precious intervals, Ian found himself surrounded by several of his clansmen determined to see him dead rather than allied to the black-haired Grant. Against the quickness and fury of Ian they had no chance even with all the odds in their favour, and he escaped to tell Iseabel of his increasing persecution. Nothing daunted, his betrothed hid him in the barn at Tulloch, but there his enemies immediately traced him, and the force was comprised of both MacGregors and Grants. It was sheer madness to resist, but at the door of that barn Ian wielded the sword while Iseabel loaded and reloaded the musket and plied her hero with words of admiration and encouragement.

There was a moment when Ian's hand faltered because Iseabel's brother was his assailant. The MacGregor's sword clashed in self-defence instead of attack, against the weapon of the man whose eyes were the colour of Iseabel's, whose features bore so strong a resemblance to the white face of the girl in the shadows.

" Kill, kill him," came the sister's firm command. " If you do not, I must. Save me from that. It is your right. 'Tis his life or yours. I choose. Kill ! " Ian obeyed, and continued to lay about him with such dexterity that at last not one man was left. The dead lay at the great barn door, a heap of mingled blood and tartan. What must Iseabel's thoughts have been as she looked at the unbidden guests of this her wedding night? The arm of her brother protruded from beneath the body of a MacGregor, its length ripped from elbow to wrist, and the blood that was kith with her own stained the dead whiteness of another Grant's face. Ian's voice full of suppressed joy called to her from the shadow of the barn, " Iseabel, that is the end of them, we are safe now, and together and alone," and in the exuberance of his victory he composed and danced then and there the now famous Reel of Tulloch.

It is right that the piper should allow that tune

to end with the wail of escaping breath, for Ian was killed soon after he had won his happiness, and when his severed head was shown to Iseabel—she who had seen so much bloodshed, who had helped to deal death and face the consequences fearlessly—Iseabel was overwhelmed with grief and died of shock. Perhaps those who buried her heard some faint echo of the famous reel.

It is not known why the Grants opposed the marriage so relentlessly, but Ian certainly had one relation who was no recommendation. One would hardly credit, on hearing this cousin described by those who saw him on trial as " a very ugly man with red hair all over his body," that he was of a personality irresistible to the ladies and that he always aroused their undisguised affections at first sight. Though his offences were many, cattle-stealing and murder among them, yet the women of Tulloch, from Castle and cottage, fell in love with this unprepossessing man. The traditional reason for their blindness is given as being due to a mole on his forehead. By just such a mysterious love-spot or gradh-seirc did Diarmuid the lover of Grainne, and Angus the Celtic Love-god, un-wittingly rouse the adoration of the world of women ; but, unlike Peter Roy MacGrigor, they avoided causing sorrow and garnering trouble, by wearing a helmet to cover the magic. Peter's admirers turned out to be of inestimable value to him, for when he was captured and sent to Edinburgh for trial, it was the ladies who offered a hundred crowns for his ransom. The second time he was forcibly taken to the capital, he did not fare so well. He could hardly expect to do so—his judges were men who saw only a very ugly man whose body was covered with red hair, and they would not have been able to understand the ladies of Tulloch who wept inconsolably at the news of his hanging.

Though there was something peculiarly fitting in the sound of the violin played in the forest, there was also a lasting satisfaction in the memory of an evening beside a blazing fire, where an old fiddler sat in a wheel-backed chair, and watched the spurting flames from the larch logs as his fingers wandered from one tune to the next, joining the melodies with little " plaints," as if a strange bird called old tunes from the past. It was winter time, and the snow piled silently on to the deep window-sill, so that when the necessity came to leave the company in the circle of fire and lamplight, the outer quiet and cold seemed manifestations of an entirely different world.

There are many varieties of silence. The complete absence of sound on a mountain top is quite unlike the conscious hush of an absorbed crowd, and the airy silence of a wood bears no relation to the crisp quiet of a small room, and the silence of snow is like none of these. It is heavy and thick, and is undisturbed by the swish and thud of falling masses as overladen boughs cast their fluffy burdens.

Snow in the forest is a scene of unforgettable beauty. Summer has its flowers, its scents, its songs; but it is worth the effort of plunging about in soft snow to see a weeping birch with every fragile twig outlined in glittering white, and behind it a giant spruce, with foliage pitch-black on the underside of boughs that bear stupendous rounded blossoms of snow. Roughness of juniper and heather become no more than snowy undulations, and tree after tree billows with cumulus clouds of snow. At such a time, Speyside is a glittering world, bespattered with shadows of brilliant blue, and there is a high note of joy in the sound of passing sleigh-runners as the produce from an outlying farm goes past on its way to the station. The skyline joins to hills that seem composed of solid snow; hills with all detail obliterated, whose corries are lit with a strange reflected light.

Evenings bring concerts and badminton matches in the village halls, and holiday afternoons find the shinty players on the fields wielding the camus, though the collecting of teams is a different matter from the days when a double number could be gathered from a single farm. Is shinty the oldest sport in Scotland, that reference to it should go right back to the days when over-enthusiastic players used the level turf before the Giant's Castle for their field, and paid the price of their temerity before they could score a hale? Many an organised Ceilidh entices the Speyside folk from their homes, but the little accidental ceilidh is the most enjoyable. Neighbours drop in unexpectedly and the talk turns to the events of past years: to the prowess of the Minister who crossed the Dow or Little Lochan at Alvie on a horse when the ice was thick; to the severe frost which allowed laden carts to cross the Spey at Boat of Garten; and to the more distant tragedy of the death of Major Rice, who was drowned when a treacherous thaw broke up the ice of Loch an Eilein. Perhaps some one remembers an old rhyme that leads to an older song, then back the word goes to anecdote again, and even the oldest story is mocked by the flame-flowers as they spring reincarnated from vegetation that has been dead these many thousand years.

I was guest on a winter's night at just such a gathering. The little cottage was so indistinct against the hillside as to seem built of the twilights. Its slates caught the last luminosity of the sky, its windows were black except for the glimmer of firelight that shot the tiny square panes like shafts of summer lightning. The Guidwife, with enough years behind her to have gathered the qualities of humour and resignation, bade me welcome and motioned me into the circle of firelight. The room was low and raftered, all one side of it occupied by two box-beds, in one of which lay her mother. The old lady was propped up on the pillows, her thin hands resting helplessly on the Clan plaid that acted as coverlet. Her scanty white hair was drawn back from her narrow forehead, and her sunken lips had grown childishly tender. Occasionally she mumbled incoherently, needing only the answer of attentive eyes to soothe her to silence ; but from the few words, seemingly as disconnected as the drops from a spigot, it was obvious that the imagery of a past day, old beliefs and forgotten legends, were accompanying her to the Dark Glen as surely as they had been her companions in life through the corries of her familiar land. Her mind was busy with tales at which moderns might scoff ; heroes too radiant and performers of deeds too iridescent to mix with common talk, though she had supped them with her porridge

THE SLUGGAN IN SNOW-TIME

(page 206)

and woven them into the stiff woof of her life's religion.

The other guests talked and sang, played the fiddle and laughed in low content.   The bedridden woman's vitality had been coming and going all year as regularly as the rising and waning of the moon, and I was the only one who felt that the big silver watch pinned to the bed-curtain ticked away the moments of ebbing life with an insistent and unrelenting impertinence.   She had outlived all her children but one, and insisted that such had been the prophecy of a Faerie whom she had met as a girl and to whom she had given a red ribbon.

Here was one freed from the commonplaces of daily life, and I thought of the varied items that had gone to the forming of her sound philosophy and refined imagination :

The height and aloofness of the hills, something from Braeriach, from Carn Eilrig and the Tor ; the whispered power of the surrounding forests ; the near feel of the tartan to illustrate the fierce tales of the past ; the wonder-purity of winter snows ; and always, always through the rich pattern of the myriad flowers of summer, the dark secret of the swirling Spey.

o

SOME BOOKS ABOUT SCOTLAND

PUBLISHED BY

ROBERT GRANT & SON

126 PRINCES STREET

EDINBURGH

THE HIGHLANDS & ISLANDS

AUTUMNS IN SKYE, ROSS AND SUTHER-LAND. By T. Ratcliffe Barnett. With 16 Illustrations and Map End-paper. Price 7s. 6d., postage 4d.

THE PEAKS, LOCHS AND COASTS OF THE WESTERN HIGHLANDS. By Arthur Gardner. New and Enlarged Edition. With 115 Illustrations from the Author's Photographs. Price 10s. 6d., postage 6d.

THE LAND OF LOCHIEL AND THE MAGIC WEST. By T. Ratcliffe Barnett. With 20 Illustrations and Map End-paper. Price 7s. 6d., postage 4d.

THE ROAD TO RANNOCH AND THE SUMMER ISLES. By T. Ratcliffe Barnett. With 16 Illustrations and Map End-paper. Price 7s. 6d., postage 4d. Cheap Edition, 5s.

THE ROAD TO THE ISLES: POETRY, LORE, AND TRADITION OF THE HEBRIDES. By Kenneth Macleod. With an Introduction by Marjory Kennedy-Fraser. With Map End-paper and Decorations. Price 7s. 6d., postage 5d.

THE BEAUTIFUL ISLE OF MULL: WITH IONA AND THE ISLE OF SAINTS. By Thomas Hannan. With 16 Illustrations from Photographs by the Author, and Map End-paper. Price 7s. 6d., postage 4d.

THE CALL OF THE ISLAND. FIVE TALES. By Charles L. Warr, Author of "The Unseen Host." Containing The Call of the Island; The Christ of the Trenches; The Death Music; The Lady of Laggan; St. Bride of the Mantle. Price 7s. 6d., postage 6d.

THE LOWLANDS

ROBERT GRANT & SON
126 PRINCES STREET, EDINBURGH
and all booksellers